MOUNTAIN BOYS
ARE FREE

For Lynn:
Your friend,
Kerr
11/15/93

MOUNTAIN BOYS ARE FREE

ARE FREE

PORTRAIT OF NED GUTHRIE,
THE MUSICIANS' ABRAHAM LINCOLN

Jim Lowe

MOUNTAIN BOYS ARE FREE

Published by James G. Lowe.
Designed by Katy Fraczek.
Cover photograph by Jim Noelker of the *Charleston Gazette*.
Back cover quotation from Jay Victor,
courtesy of *Nation's Labor*.

Printed by Haddon Craftsmen, Inc., Scranton, PA

® GCIU

Made in the United States of America.

Library of Congress Catalog Card Number 92-83938
ISBN 0-9635197-0-0
1 3 5 7 9 10 8 6 4 2
1993

JAMES G. LOWE
P. O. BOX 1221
NEVADA CITY
CA 95959
USA

Acknowledgments

While gathering information for Ned Guthrie's story, there was only one person who withheld comment, and then only for legal reasons. Everyone bent over backwards, and I am grateful for the stories, information, and help given me by:

My sweetheart and printing consultant Katy Fraczek; teacher Steve Green; teacher Eugene Ham; writer Mark Hubbard; librarian Ed Tyson; writer-editor Michael Brackney; copy editor and percussionist Kit Bailey; indexer Jan Rubiales; attorney Gary J. Cogley; pianist Bob Bellezza; photographer Gail S. Rebhan; Jane Rosinski of Mattox Photography; artist Tom Brown; artist Bill Ham (who provided the brush and ink image for my logo).

And Anne and Heber Pittman; West Virginia Secretary of State Ken Hechler; Charleston AFL-CIO writer-editor Lee Beard; writers Nancy Adams and Lori Henshey of the West Virginia Division of Culture and History; culturalist and humanitarian Norman Fagen; music store owner Dave

Herbert, Jr.; attorney George Daugherty; writer-editor Topper Sherwood; jazz trumpeter Jim Beane; Ned Guthrie's Secretary Fran Beane; Circuit Court Judge Todd Kaufman; Benjamin H. Caldwell, Jr., M.D., P.C.; attorney Brian Moir.

And President Mark T. Massagli and the offices of the American Federation of Musicians; now deceased unionist Kelly Castleberry; unionist Ray Hair; unionist and artist Shorty Vest; retired unionist Ted Rube "Thumbs" Dreyer; retired unionist Henry "Hank" Armantrout; the AFL-CIO's Department of Professional Employees.

And the soldiers of knowledge at the Nevada City Library; the Grass Valley Library; the Nevada County Library; the Nevada County Law Library; the Auburn-Placer County Library; the California State Library; the San Francisco Law Library; writer and librarian Samuel Brylowski of the Motion Picture, Broadcasting, and Recorded Sound Division at the Library of Congress.

And Assistant Editor Debby Jackson of *Goldenseal;* Managing Editor Jessica Roe of the *International Musician;* Jay Victor of *Nation's Labor;* Christian Angermann of the *Daily News;* photographer Jim Noelker of the *Charleston Gazzette; Broadcasting, Broadcast Advertising.*

And also Diane Virginia (Guthrie) Mitchel; Ned Guthrie, Jr.; Gladys Virginia Guthrie; and Ned Humphries Guthrie himself—all helped bring the following story to life on paper.

*Dedicated
to the memory of
Roy Labon Pittman,
Kelly L. Castleberry II,
and to an era
when live music had a place
in the hearts and minds
of the American people.*

Necessary to the telling of Ned Guthrie's story is the musicians' side of their old, but continuing, dispute with the broadcasters. No pretense was made by the author to provide a balanced presentation.

Contents

PART III

PART I

Mountain People

We are mountain people.
We are a boorish set, they tell us—
Hard-bitten, coarse of feature and of speech,
Shallow and brawling as the mountain streams,
With morale friable as our sandstone.

All my life I have wanted to tell them:
That we are mountain people,
That mountain streams have pools of deep quietness,
And that beneath the sandstone of our hills
There is granite.

—Leonard L. Tate

(COURTESY OF RUTH TATE COOK AND CLARA BELLE BOWDEN)

The Young West Virginian

Ned's story begins in Charleston, West Virginia on the Ninth Day of May in Nineteen Hundred and Ten. His parents, Robert Fleetwood Guthrie and Helen "Goldie" Maloy—both of Scottish origin—married, divorced, and at age five, Ned (with a degree of puzzlement) attended their second marriage ceremony—then saw them divorced again the next year.

Robert and Goldie usually left Ned at the Plaza Theatre on Saturday afternoons. It was a vaudeville house with a seven-piece pit orchestra. They separated the orchestra from the theatre seats with a brass rail. Ned always sat in the first row, leaning forward over the rail to catch every move of the drummer—his name was Cam Matthews—and the way he hit the cues and the rickyticks and the cymbal hits. It fascinated Ned. An alert child, ever curious, he needed to know what made a sound. When he heard somebody talking, he insisted on knowing what was being said.

Robert enlisted in the United States Marine Corps and,

when Goldie took a job at the Elk Bank, Ned was shuffled off to a boarding school "out in the sticks."

In 1917, there were few roads to Grundy Presbyterian School in Buchannan County, Virginia. Students stayed there from the beginning of the school term in September until school was out in June. It was the middle of June before Ned could find a ride out of Grundy to spend his short summer vacation with his mother. To make matters worse, as a short seven-year-old boy in a coeducational school, he was stuck in the *girls'* dormitory. Though small, Ned Humphries Guthrie was verbal. He complained, but says, "That's the way it was in Grundy."

Something happened to Ned there at Grundy that had a profound religious impact on him throughout his life. Construction gangs were building a railroad across the Pike Branch of the Big Sandy River, working about the distance of one and one-half football fields from the school. Ned had drawn a little ring in the clay and was practicing marbles. Some bigger boys up on the veranda in the main campus screamed, "FIRE IN THE HOLE! FIRE IN THE HOLE!" Ned didn't know what that meant, but he ran up on the porch seconds before a crew shot off a blast of dynamite, lobbing a rock the size of a basketball high into the air. It sailed in a perfect arch over Pike Fork—then smashed in the exact spot where Ned had been squatting. "I'd heard an awful lot about God, you know," Ned still insists, "and that was more than just luck!"

An engineer named Mont J. Carmack took an interest in Goldie, and they soon wed. Ned called him "Father Mack," and the two of them got along famously. Father Mack was an organization-minded man who had built eighteen miles of railroad to a coal site, and brought electricity to the town of Covington, Virginia. He and his father bought a horse-drawn streetcar company in Charleston, then electrified it. Among his many endeavors, Carmack served intermittently as Secretary and Chaplain to the Kiwanis Club in Charleston for thirty-five years. He disapproved of unions, and showing himself as a strong company man, Carmack carried around two pearl-handled Smith & Wesson revolvers when he was out in the field. Ned later inherited them.

Ned's new found home suffered the worst of calamities. When he was ten years old his mother fell ill with tubercular pleurisy, and was hospitalized some two hundred miles from home, at Terra Alta. Laden with gifts, Ned and Mack went to spend three or four days with her at Christmas time. Goldie wanted to go home with them, but she was held over for tests—which revealed that her condition was complicated by stomach cancer.

Mack fetched her on a Monday afternoon in January, and brought her home on a cot in the baggage car of a Baltimore & Ohio Railroad trunk line. On the following Thursday her pulse weakened, and she called Ned to her bedside to say plaintively and *oh so directly*, "I'm going to leave you and die."

"Mother you can't!" cried Ned.

"Well, it's going to be that way. When I'm gone, go live with your grandparents. You are a Guthrie."

The following day, with her head resting on Mack's shoulder, her cheek pressed against his, Goldie passed away. Ned got a white rose and put it in her hand. Despite the hard times, only on her deathbed had Ned's mother willingly given up her pride to hand her son over to the Guthries.

Helen had been born in 1893 in Middleport, Ohio, just across the Ohio River from West Virginia. She came from a family of railroad workers named Richardson but was raised by the Maloys, another railroad family. They adopted her after her parents separated—so at age ten, she went to live with them in South Charleston in a company house perched high on a steep bank overlooking the tracks of the Chesapeake & Ohio Railroad.

Helen became an expert horsewoman by age fifteen. One day, on a dare, she rode her horse up the long, steep stairway leading up to the back door of her foster father's house. Then, when the horse got scared and wouldn't go back down those stairs, she lead her horse through the house—out the front door to ground level—and caught *hell* for it. Helen was a popular girl, a good basketball player who played the organ and did Red Cross work during World War I. She enjoyed riding her horse up and down Charleston Street, and seeing her with her long golden hair almost every day—the locals nicknamed her "Goldie."

Ned would have preferred to stay with Father Mack, but his father (who was his legal guardian) and his grandparents were anxious to have him. Although it was done in a friendly way, in a letter to Goldie's cousin, Matilda, Carmack wrote, "I will keep my eye on him, too, and do all I can to see that he grows into the man his mother tried so hard to make him."

Ned's father was sent to France with the Marines' 5th Regiment in 1919. The family decided to send Ned to another boarding school, this time the Allegheny Collegiate Institute—a military school in Alderson, West Virginia.

The Guthrie family had a military tradition. From Scotland to the New World came three brothers of the Guthrie Clan (*gu thrie* means "good three" in Old Scottish). Arriving sometime prior to the American Revolution, one brother settled his family on the eastern shore of Maryland, and the others traveled through Pennsylvania, then ventured into the interior of western Virginia.[1] At least one-half of them settled in the Kanawha Valley, and some of the remaining Guthries later pushed west into Oklahoma territory. Guthries joined the rebel frontiersmen in the Virginia Militia, and fought against the English in the Battle of King's Mountain, a decisive rebel victory. For their military service, they were awarded approximately five land tracts in the Kanawha Valley by the new American government.

Ned's father was born in 1890 out in a rural hamlet called "Guthrie," where there was a Guthrie Post Office. Guthries, in fact, had once owned all the area from Slip Hill (about two miles from West Washington Street) over to what is named Kanawha Two Mile (for the creek that enters the Kanawha River two miles down from the Elk River)—in the center of Charleston. During World War II, the family name was chosen for the Air Force Base that was established to provide radar to protect the chemical production plants in the Kanawha Valley.

Ned was beginning his second year at Alderson when he received word that his father had returned from France as a *war hero,* and was scheduled to conduct an inspection of Ned's company. (His school had only one company, and he had a rifle that stood taller than he did—an old Spanish-American War piece weighing twelve pounds.) On the big day, Ned's company fell in and Sergeant Robert Guthrie, in full Marine dress complete with decorations, conducted the inspection in true military fashion. Standing tall, so young and impressionable, Ned felt himself to be the proudest boy in the world. He never forgot how his daddy instilled patriotism in him.

During World War I, Ned's father had been sent into the thick of battle. Germans launched a massive counter-attack on the Western Front in the summer of 1918, and Robert's outfit was to advance over a bridge into a forest filled with German soldiers—even as French troops were in full retreat suffering twenty-five percent casualties. French troops were hollering "RETREAT! RETREAT!" Marines took up the call,

7

ROBERT FLEETWOOD GUTHRIE

HELEN "GOLDIE" MALOY
PHOTOGRAPH BY EXHIBIT STUDIO

MONT J. CARMACK
PHOTOGRAPH BY GRABELY & MOORE

GOLDIE, NED,
AND FATHER MACK

A SUNDAY AUTOMOBILE DRIVE

"RETREAT, HELL! WE JUST GOT HERE!" They advanced, suffering seventy-five percent casualties in one battle alone. Germans named them "Devil Dogs." They fought at Belleau Woods (referred to as the Gettysburg of that war) and in the Battle of Chateau Thierry. One week before the Armistice, Robert fell in the Battle of the Argonne Forest. He once told Ned, "Shells came over and exploded, and I couldn't get my gas mask on fast enough—*that* time." He inhaled a combination of Phosgene and mustard gas, and the fighting was so intense that it was three days before stretcher bearers could get to him. Blinded for fifteen days, his eyes would be red and teared some twenty years later. His left lung was completely burned-out with scar tissue, and the enamel on his teeth went bad. He spent six months in a French hospital recuperating, and returned home with tuberculosis. Before leaving for America, Robert was awarded the *Croix de Guerre* with two palms—the French Government's highest award. (The Marines honored him fifty years later.)

Robert never had any money, to speak of, and his disabilities didn't help matters. His financial status differed greatly from that of his brothers, LaMont and George, the successful founders of the Guthrie Morris Campbell Company (a wholesale dry goods business). "But that wasn't us," Ned makes clear, "and West Virginia was in a depression years before the market crash of 1929. During that time, all you knew was hard and just keep tryin'."

Soon after his return from France, Robert met and married Lela Yvonne Lucas, a young girl from Hurricane, West Virginia. Only nine years older than Ned, Lela won his heart when she bucked the Guthries (Ned's uncles, aunts *and* grandmother) who were all bent on his return to military school. Lela put her foot down, and asserted that she would "take Ned and he can stay with his Dad and me." And that's what she did.

Robert moved his family out of Charleston to Morgantown, and Ned entered sixth grade there. Much to his delight his homeroom teacher played the piano and often cranked up the Victrola (with the morning glory horn on it). Ned remembers being enchanted by the rhythm and melody of "Tales of Hoffman." He learned to love classical music, and badly wanted piano lessons.

A piano teacher lived directly across the street from Ned's house, but Robert didn't see how he could pay fifty cents per lesson. So instead, he bought Ned a good wooden tenor snare drum for twenty dollars, along with two fine ebony drumsticks that cost one dollar each. Ned was happy. He and another boy played their drums to accompany Mrs. Leets, the school principal. She played piano for the morning's march into class—a ritual that got Ned interested in playing.

Robert entered into a vocational program for disabled veterans in 1923 (a forerunner of the GI Bill of Rights)—necessitating another family move—this time to Point Pleasant. He received a federal grant for an experimental strawberry project, and gave Ned one-fifth of an acre to till.

Living in Morgantown close to West Virginia University, Ned met an older boy named Fuzzy Knight, a "live wire" cheerleader for the football team. These were championship years for this University, and Fuzzy had distinguished himself by writing the school's "Fight, Fight, Fight, Fight Mountaineer" song. Ned started following him to games, and became the unofficial "tag-along" mascot of the team. To show what WVU planned to do to the opposing team the next day, the engineering students started dressing him up, parading him around on a stretcher at pep rallies. Far from being embarrassed by it, Ned says, "Those kinds of things just seemed commonplace with me. They were undefeated under

Coach Spears, and I happened to be at the right place at the right time to try and get some publicity. And, I developed an alertness which helped me all through my life."

Ned kept himself busy selling newspapers, and went out for football at Point Pleasant High School. At one hundred and thirty-five pounds, however, he had a bruised and brief career on the gridiron, so he went to join the band—snare drum and ebony sticks in hand.

"We don't need any drummers," said the band director, "but I can let you have a good, used clarinet for twenty-five dollars."

Ned asked, "What's a clarinet?"

As he grew strawberries to buy his way into the band, Ned could hear calliopes on the excursion steamboats traveling up and down the Ohio River, only one-half of a mile away from his home. He daydreamed about playing music on those boats, and when he sold twenty-five dollars worth of strawberries he anxiously reported to the band director to claim his chair in the band. Ned thinks of it as the first true home he ever found (not that everything was always hunky-dory).

On one tacky occasion the band director ordered them out on a river steamboat cruise on the *Chris Greene* to nearby Gallipolis, Ohio. They picked up Williams Jennings Bryan, known for his oratory, and played all the way back to Point Pleasant—then on to the courthouse to play some more, like a kind of marathon. Bryan droned on about the virtue of John W. Davis (the 1924 presidential candidate from West Virginia).

"The director was paid fifty dollars. And what did we get?" asks Ned. *"Gee,* don't you want a boat ride? Don't you want to feel *important?"*

During summer vacation there was a more dramatic incident when the director contacted all of the band members and told them to bring their instruments and uniforms and to meet at the school at dusk. He didn't say where they were going to play and, on the way over to "wherever," it got pitch dark. There was no moon at all, but Ned, driving his dad's 1924 flatbed Ford with the lights off, could tell by the curves in the road where he was being led. He was sure of it when they told him to stop and park, and they all walked down a bank into a ball park. They could hear voices and cars driving into the area without lights. The director called "Activity," a march they all knew by heart, to begin when the lights came on. Suddenly, a twenty-foot cross on the pitcher's mound burst into flames illuminating the ball diamond. The band found themselves at first base, and all around the diamond in a circle were hooded figures—*the Ku Klux Klan!* Some of them were on horseback. All of the kids were scared. Ned got angry too, but he crammed it into his craw. He wanted to leave, but he didn't dare.

After it was over Ned was back at the wheel of his dad's flatbed, with his cousin Paul Guthrie in the back bouncing around with the equipment. Ned drove about a quarter of a mile, then turned on his lights. Fully absorbed in his angry drive home, he was traveling through a meadow following ruts in the ground when Paul screamed, "STOP! STOP! THE KU KLUX IS COMIN' AFTER US!" Ned looked in the rear-view mirror and saw him—a Klansman on a horse trying to get around the truck. It scared Ned and he slammed on the brakes. The horse also had a hood over her eyes, and there was a big **THONK!** when she hit the truck bed. The rider came sailing over the side of the truck and landed beside the left front wheel. He groaned, as the horse whinnied and neighed in pain and galloped off. When Ned saw that he was down, he stepped on the gas and got the hell out of there. He and Paul had nightmares for weeks after that, because they didn't know if that guy was chasing them or not. They did know who they were dealing with, and the whole thing was a "turn-off" to Ned. He contends, "It was just plain exploitation—racial, and un-American. And I was uncomfortable with that!"

DRAWING BY SHORTY VEST

When the agricultural economy worsened in West Virginia, Robert lost his land. In 1925, he had to move his family back to Charleston. Ned took along the muskmelons he had raised in order to buy an alto saxophone, and when they got to Charleston he sold them for seventy-seven dollars. Then, lo and behold, he found a good, used alto for seventy-five bucks. His dad also got lucky and landed a job working for the U.S. Government. Things were looking up.

16

The following year Ned entered Charleston High School, and easily qualified to become a charter member of the school band that was starting up. Having already learned how to read music and play clarinet and sax at the schools he had attended, he began his training for the music profession under an able and stern Englishman—a true musician— named J. Henry Francis. Director Francis had formed the band and taught orchestra, glee club, and chorus at Charleston High for some twenty-five years.

Director Francis was known for taking advantage of everything he could that would benefit his students. When he heard that John Philip Sousa was bringing his band to Charleston, he worked a deal for Sousa to guest conduct the school band for just one selection at intermission time. In exchange, the band members would serve as ushers in their uniforms which, according to Ned, made them look like Russian sailors.

The man who was called "The March King" had a world famous sixty-two piece band—the best! Ned sat in the first clarinet chair and his friend, Charley Hanna, their first trumpet player, sat in Sousa's lead chair spot. They were thrilled. Ned says, "Sousa was to people then like Elvis Presley was to his generation, like Kenny Rogers to his, and like Louis Armstrong was to my generation. We didn't fill up half the seats on stage, but we had practiced 'El Capitan'—it's probably the easiest of the Sousa marches—for weeks and weeks.

"When Sousa came out there, I hadn't seen him except from the floor. But he stepped up on a little box, because he was very short—a diminutive person. And he stood on the podium, with the music stand in front of him. He picked up the baton real quickly and said, 'Good afternoon, gentlemen,' then came down with the stick. And we all missed it, except Charley Hanna and Lawrence McClain, the bass drummer. They played the introduction, just trumpet and bass drum. But it took seven or eight bars for the band to catch up, because with Sousa, you didn't stop. It was the *last* downbeat I ever missed."

Ned immersed himself in musical study and practice. In addition to his school studies, he took thirty clarinet lessons from a teacher named George Crumb. Crumb piloted Ned through the change in fingering from the Albert System to the Boehm System.

When he was fifteen years old, Ned fibbed about his age to enlist in the 150th Infantry National Guard, stationed in Charleston, the capital city. He wanted to play in the Regimental Band led by German-born Professor Manch. Under Manch, Ned learned to produce a broad German tone on his instrument.

At this time, the Marines were fighting the controversial "Banana Wars" in Latin America, and it was rumored that the 150th Regiment would be sent to Nicaragua. Ned was happy about that. *After all,* he thought, *I was in military school for one year.* It turned out to be a false alarm. They didn't go. Instead, they went troopin' out, marching the drill units back to their Summer encampment to retire the colors.

One day on the way out, they were playing "The Black Horse Troop," a spirited march that didn't feature brass instruments—only clarinets, flutes, and "peckhorns" (instruments one couldn't hear two blocks away). A regular army "chicken colonel" Regimental Commander Stacy came riding up on his steed "all spit 'n' fire" demanding, "What kind of march is *that?* Who's in charge of this band?"

Warrant Officer Richmond Houston replied, "I am, Sir."

"Who wrote that march?" probed the colonel.

"Sousa, Sir," replied Houston.

"I don't give a *damn* who wrote it!" bellowed the Commander. "Don't play it under my command! Can't hear it! Play somethin' you can hear! And you don't have a cymbal player. Where *is* he?"

"We don't have a cymbal player, Sir," answered Houston.

"Well, take one of those trumpet players or clarinet players over there and give 'em some cymbals!" ordered Colonel Stacy.

Ned figured that this was a fine time to work in his cousin Paul Guthrie, and telephoned that evening to invite him. When Paul replied, "I don't know anything about music," Ned told him, "Well, let me tell ya' I'm acting supply sergeant, and I can get you the cymbals. And you join the band, get a uniform, carry a pistol—do it all! All you have to do is march beside that bass drum 'n' watch 'em. Every time he hits the bass drum with that stick beater, you bang those cymbals. Let him do the readin'." Paul enlisted to join the band, and so began his military career. (In 1929, he was transferred into a machine gun company, and was deeply disgruntled about it. Some of the Guthries had a talk with Paul. Whatever was said, during World War II Paul rapidly advanced up through the ranks, the hard way, to become a full-fledged brigadier general—and received a Silver Star Medal for capturing a town behind German lines.)

The Regimental Band went on a trip to Williamson, the county seat of Mingo County, situated next to the Kentucky border. They went by special railroad coaches, and set up barracks on the third floor of the Court House. They took out the courtroom furniture to make way for army cots, and, as soon as they were settled, two legionnaires came up the stairs with a brand new washtub with about four inches in it— enough good moonshine to keep them "happified" for days. Ned enjoyed it, even though they twice got them up in the middle of the night to parade up and down a mountain side. They were busy making an impression, trying to elect a local commander to the state unit of the American Legion. "It's another form of exploitation, I always thought," reflects Guthrie. "They had us going to conventions of the American Legion and other political things. The Government paid for it, and we got one dollar a day army pay. That's how the military musicians are regarded by the 'brass'."

When Ned graduated from high school in the Class of 1927, he was itching to get on the road with a band. An opportunity to do just that afforded itself, but Uncle George Guthrie appeared with a job offer. He wanted Ned to go to work in a wholesale grocery house, an office and sales job. Ned pleaded with him saying, "If you want to help me, help me go to college. I want to study music."

"No. You don't want that," replied Uncle George. "You meet me here Monday morning. We're going to Rainelle. We're going to get you a job!"

Thus, two weeks after his graduation, Ned reluctantly went to work for eighty-five dollars per month at the New River Grocery Company, located eighty miles from Charleston in the Appalachian Mountains.

It wasn't long, however, until Ned detected an opportunity. Soon after he started working in Rainelle, he met a man named Smitty Holsberry. Smitty worked as a distributor for the Standard Oil Company. Smitty also had a set of drums and a piano-playing wife. Their friend, Bern Dobbins, played banjo and owned an alto saxophone made of ebonite. Ned hunted up a bass player and formed the Midland Trail Five—so named for the gig he got on U.S. Route 60 (the road that runs from Norfolk, Virginia over the Blue Ridge and the Allegheny Mountains, across the Great Plains, and over the Rockies and through deserts to San Diego, California).

They worked Lee's Tree Tavern, situated at the highest point on this route, about one hundred yards from the great white oak on a bald knob where General Lee had his Civil War headquarters. At an altitude of 3,420 feet above sea level, people sometimes slogged through three and four feet of snow to drink their moonshine whiskey and dance at Lee's Tree Tavern.

Its owner, John Goff, also owned the Pioneer Theatre where he showed silent films. Ned worked there with a piano player named Charley Jeeter, a good musician who, like Ned, was stuck with a day gig. His was as a dispatcher on the Shea Locomotive mountain spur railroad that hauled chestnut logs to a sawmill. Together with two other musicians they played the musical scores that accompanied the silent movies. Behind the silver screen, Goff and his sons were in charge of the sound effects.

One evening they were playing the score to *The Big Parade,* a war movie about the Battle at the Forest of the Argonne, where Ned's father had been wounded. As the battle progressed (Ned playing clarinet on bugle calls and charges) the band worked itself up into a frenzy of sound with Goff's boys extemporizing the sounds of war. Looming on the screen were French Whippet tanks (in real life about the size of a van) wreaking havoc with the Kaiser's forces. For tank sounds, Goff had two oil barrels with logging chains in them—turning them over and over with a loud rumble. Then they started imitating artillery fire—*by shooting off shotguns* behind screen. Smoke billowed into the pit, and the band could barely continue playing. Truly "touched" by the performance, the first three rows of people got up and left, choking on the smoke. Guthrie says, "You'd just improvise."

Back at Lee's Tree Tavern Ned was charging two dollars at the door, and one night returned home with fifty-eight dollars, his share for the evening. That was a considerable amount of money in the 1920's, and it decided the issue for Ned. He knew what he wanted to do with his life—and it wasn't figuring out wholesale orders in a grocery house—so he asked for a raise. (Few workers of any variety were pushing their bosses for raises in West Virginia in 1928.) Taking the bait, the store manager gave him a prompt "NO!" Ned replied, "Okay," and loosening his tie, he smiled and moved in the direction of the door, adding, "I'm through today. I've enjoyed it."

He decided to join his musician friends at the New River State College in Montgomery, West Virginia, and hitchhiked the eighty miles back to Charleston to ask his father for tuition money. Robert was almost broke, but he gave him ten dollars. That wasn't much of a college start, but Ned was already an accomplished musician—*and* a talker. He talked his way into a scholarship with the president of the college. In exchange for tuition, room and board, plus fifty dollars thrown in each semester, Ned was to play at all school functions, from sporting events to glee club concerts, including Wednesday night dances in the gymnasium with the Campus Boys Dance Band.

He made additional money teaching clarinet, and began working with the Faymont Hotel Orchestra in Montgomery. It was a ten-piece band with a library led by trumpeter Harry Bowman, and featured Joe Drasnin on stand-up fiddle. Ned also worked for two dollars per night accompanying silent films in the pit band at the Avalon Theatre. With all this moonlighting, some college people became concerned, and were poised to reprimand Ned—but he kept his grades up and honored his commitments.

Professor Edwin H. Peters, a graduate of the Chicago Conservatory of Music, was Ned's band instructor. He was close to his students, although he was bigger and older—with a cigar tucked in the corner of his mouth. One day Peters caught Ned in the hall and challenged, "Do you think you can

play? You come after class and we'll play some duets." Ned
showed up and unpacked his alto sax. As he got out the
Universal Music Book that had duets in it, he noticed that
Peters was unpacking a tenor sax. Ned remarked, "That ain't
no tenor part. That's an alto part!"

Peters's eyes lit up as he instructed, "Well, you just start
playing. I'll play *your* book."

They later switched parts and Ned learned transposition.
He admits that he never got as good as was Peters, who surely
made him try.

A talented trumpet player named Wayland Redden and
Ned started up a combo they named the Campus Cats, but
when a job opened up back in Charleston for a lead sax man
at the Kearse Theatre Ballroom, Ned decided to quit school.
He played with Charley Giles and his Vagabonds, and couldn't
pass up such an opportunity to play with professional musicians. Later on they worked on the *Edward's Moonlight,* an
excursion dance boat on the Kanawha River.

Though Ned had snapped up first chair in a fine band, and
his dreams were coming true, Robert wasn't happy about Ned
quitting school. He wanted him to try out for Annapolis, so to
keep the peace, Ned took on another job as an usher at the
Kearse Theatre. He kept that up for six months, but by then
he wanted to get on the road so bad he could taste it.

The panic bands of the Depression Era generally changed personnel and luck three times each year: at the end of the spring season on Memorial Day—when musicians planned summer gigs somewhere that usually started in the month of June; on Labor Day—the end of the summer season; and in January. A paltry form of security was to be found in motion. Going home was defeat.

On the Road

There was a drummer named Spraque Bollingen working with Ned in the Vagabonds. Spraque also played with a ragtime jazz band in Kentucky, and he sparked Ned's musical career in November of 1929 by getting Ned and banjoist named Glen Baker a job with "Del Willis and his Kentucky Wildcats." So they "split" for the hills of Kentucky, to the town of Harlan—about as close to the Cumberland Gap as you can get.

Working with "Del Willis and his Kentucky Wildcats" introduced Ned to striped English walking trousers, pearl grey vests, Oxford cutaways, and patent leather shoes with grey spats. Ten strangers dressed in tuxedos—musicians or not—were indeed an alien spectacle in the southern coal fields of Kentucky. They traveled—playing inns, clubs, and some live broadcasts on a little 50 watt radio station located over a drug store in Harlan.

Then there were subscription dances. Ned was shocked that so many young people in attendance suffered from

"Jakeleg," an affliction (caused from drinking Jamaica ginger) that left a limping paralysis in their ankles. But these were high parties—where they drank moonshine whiskey, had gun tables, and what Ned assessed to be good taste in music.

In the spring, Willis took his Wildcats to Big Stone Gap, Virginia. They drove fifty miles over dirt and gravel roads to get there, and found a wooden platform, a string of lights, and an upright piano. As they climbed on the stage to start setting-up, Willis asked the promoter, "Well, where are the chairs? We can't play without somethin' to sit on."

"Oh," he replied, "I'll go get 'em and bring 'em here." They figured the promoter was a good guy and offered to help him, but he said he could handle it. Guthrie notes, "That was the first week in May of 1930—and that guy hasn't come back with those chairs yet!"

This job had been booked months ahead, and the band had been counting on the money to get them to Wilmington, North Carolina and to Carolina Beach in time for Decoration Day. To boost their meager finances, Ned himself had hustled some gigs at the Old Armory in Charleston and the Shrine Club at Mount Hope in West Virginia, and what they made, plus what they would have made in Big Stone Gap, would have been enough money to get them to North Carolina. The Wildcats had started out as an open shop band, taking whatever they could get in the way of money—but Ned had HAD IT! He told Willis that he and some of the others would quit if they all didn't get into the musicians' union. In circumstances like these, they could have the Union collect the money from the promoter, and wouldn't have to double-back or appear in court. They wouldn't always get the money, but the club could be put on the Unfair List, and have to make-do without music. The boys joined the Charleston Local, and Guthrie brags that his union card has been paid up, on time, since May 19th of 1930.

These jazz musicians were *good,* and enthusiastically re-ceived wherever they performed. They did get to Carolina Beach, and Ned was moved from lead to third chair alto sax, making room for Bill Arnold who came down from Radio Station WBT in Charlotte. Ned learned free vibrato from him. Willis had Woody Woodruff from Lexington, Kentucky on drums. As was the vogue of the day (before the silky sounds of string bass and guitar), he filled out his rhythm section with a banjoist and a sousaphonist—Glenn Baker from Charles-ton, West Virginia and Cal Martin from Gadsen, Alabama. Willis's first chair trumpet position was filled by Bob Williams from Little Rock, Arkansas, who also sang and wrote special dance arrangements. On second trumpet was Dodge Cecil from Hazard, Kentucky.

On a musical "cloud" the bandsmen left the business end of things to Del Willis. He acquired a band manager, working on a percentage basis, who rented a pavilion on Carolina Beach. It was an instant success! These Wildcats played to a full dance floor for weeks, but on the Fourth of July their manager celebrated the holiday weekend by claiming its proceeds, and was never seen again. A disgusted Del Willis soon wandered off, abandoning a dedicated group of musicians who believed in their music.

They stuck together under the name of the Kentucky Wildcats. Their immediate need for a place to stay was met by a friendly owner of the Baines Hotel, where they exchanged music for rooms and meals for two weeks until they landed a gig in nearby White Lake, North Carolina. After picking up a good piano player there named Bob Mason, to take Willis's place, they traveled to Charley Johnson's home town of Hazard, Kentucky. His family owned a Coca Cola bottling company—so the Wildcats bought army cots, bunked out in the loft of the plant, and practiced.

The area around Harlan and Hazard was well-heeled, but it wasn't an every night entertainment place. They ended up renting the Sunset Inn, located about sixteen miles east of Lexington, as a recuperative business venture. It didn't pan out, though, so Cal Martin made a concessionary telephone call to a bandleader in Erie, Pennsylvania named Mark Goff. He came to Kentucky and liked what he heard, incorporated the Wildcats into his orchestra, and called it, "Mark Goff and his Wonder Orchestra." Ned jokes that Mark used to wonder what it was all about, but Goff got them working. He transported the band to New York State where they auditioned at the Palais Royal in Buffalo, which in turn landed them bookings at the Waldemere Ballroom on Lake Erie and the State Ballroom in Erie, Pennsylvania. Goff then moved the band to the southern coal fields for the winter. Ned's roommate, trumpeter Dodge Cecil, fell ill and was hospitalized in Mount Hope, West Virginia. He died there, and Goff replaced him with Bruno Guzik, from Pittsburgh, Pennsylvania. The band endured the rest of the winter traveling through the Appalachian territory of Tennessee, Virginia, Kentucky, and West Virginia.

While staying at the Matz Hotel (one of the many hotels catering to traveling entertainers in the days of vaudeville) the Wonder Orchestra got their first break—a job playing for "the elite" at the plush Richmond Hotel in Virginia. This was a chance for national exposure, involving remote broadcasts on WRVA, a 50,000 watt station picked up by a network. On the very day that they were packed and ready to board the band bus, Ned was called to the telephone. It was his father, absolutely beaming, saying, "I have *great* news!"

Ned thought, *Oh, no!*

"Senator Hatfield has given you an appointment to take the examination for the Naval Academy at Annapolis," announced Robert.

"My gawd Daddy," gasped Ned, "I can't do that! We're booked in Richmond."

"You're crazy! This is an appointment to the Naval Academy," insisted Robert. "Look, you went to college and took the right courses. You studied in high school, and I've been in the Marines. We've talked about this for ten years. And now you're not going to *go*? If you—"

"I just can't *do* it, Daddy," broke in Ned. "We're going to go to Richmond, and we'll be broadcasting nationwide!"

Retired Marine Sergeant Robert Fleetwood Guthrie—now or soon-to-be the West Virginia State Commander of the Disabled American Veterans, also Adjutant of the John Brawley Post of the American Legion of Charleston, *and* the State Quartermaster of the Veterans of Foreign Wars—was, to say the least, upset with his son. Ned couldn't, or at least didn't, go home for well over one year. He knew that he had broken his daddy's heart—but he got on the band bus and stayed with music.

After his run with the Wonder Orchestra, in 1931 Ned went to hear the Jan Campbell Orchestra. It was the best band he had ever heard, with a fine trumpet player named Wayland Redden (his old buddy from the Campus Cats at college). He was from the Red Nichols' school of playing, and having a friend in the band—one who could play his "axe"—prompted Ned to join.

Jan Campbell was from Beckley, West Virginia, and under contract with Amusement Service Corporation (ASC). He offered Ned a tryout gig in Beckley, promising him much work up in New England and New York State. Ned passed his audition with flying colors, and learned that Jan's word was good. They traveled so much that all the band members received mail through ASC's main office on Broadway in New York City. Leaning heavily on stage stunts, it was one of the "funny hat bands" that provided on stage entertainment, such as simulating a circus—complete with seals, apes, and what Ned writes off as "the whole bit." Jan's featured attraction was a tall and gorgeous blond flapper named Peaches Browning. Peaches had sued a politician whose exploitation of her had become a national scandal. With her assets, Jan couldn't resist trying her out to see if she had a draw. She did, so Jan worked the Finger Lakes of New York State with Peaches. Peaches's featured song was "Everything's Peaches With Me." Whatever worked, Jan's band was a tremendous success. At Carsonia Park in Redding, Pennsylvania, Ned saw the big pagoda on the mountain, Campbell's name advertised on the front of streetcars, and all of forty-four hundred dancers on one *big* dance floor.

Guthrie later became involved with the Teapot Dome Scandal Headquarters in Columbus, Ohio, working with the Sinclair Oil Band. Some executive's hot idea required him to pump gas in a service station. That was "for the birds" as far as Ned was concerned, so he headed out for greener pastures.

Carl England hired him to play in his orchestra at the Venus Restaurant in Washington, D.C. During this gig he ran into a sax player from Charleston, West Virginia named Ross Pierson. Ross got Ned into Paul Graham's "Graham Crackers" in Gainesville, Florida, the first big-name band with which Ned was associated. It was handled by the Music Corporation of America (MCA)—ASC's rival.

Every year MCA booked them at the Yacht Club in St. Petersburg Beach and at the Standard Club in Atlanta, Georgia, a Jewish country club, where they played ten gigs for ten different families during Hanukkah. They also worked the Convention Hall in Atlantic City, one of the largest assembly and ballrooms in the country.

In Florida they broadcast three times each week on Radio Station WRUF, operated by Paul's brother. Every fall, busy as they were, they felt like they were biding their time—waiting for the Floridian Hotel in Miami Beach to open the winter season. Ned would soon work choice show jobs in gaming casinos in Miami and the Jacksonville and Savannah Beaches, but in 1932, the Floridian was "a first" for him. It was quite an operation. To break even on the casino alone, seventy-five thousand dollars had to be generated in play each night. This is where Ned learned to work three shows in a day.

In the days before Las Vegas existed, the Floridian was frequented by many gamblers who were big-time celebrities from both New York and Hollywood. They mostly gravitated to a section of the casino located a few doors behind the bandstand. Ned and other musicians never did get into that area. Owners and special guests had a reserved table located near the bandstand, and an odd array of personalities sat there, one of whom was "Slapsy" Maxie Rosenbloom, the heavyweight pugilist. Ned saw him do something that a great many gamblers would like to do, but couldn't—an iron *fist* to the iron jaw of a one-armed bandit! A frequent guest was Jack Benny. He was vacationing with his wife and her twin sister. (Ned had seen Benny once before in a vaudeville show at the Palace Theatre on Broadway, when Benny was relatively unknown and doing stand-up bits.) One night the guest table more or less took over the "joint." They were big tippers when they were "on a roll" and all fourteen Crackers got a "taste." At one point in the evening, the table sent Jack Benny up to the bandstand to sit in, so the fiddler surrendered his violin to Benny—the comedian.

"I will never forget it," remembers Guthrie. "The lights and everything right down on our music, and I played lead sax (in the first row). Benny was standing there saying, 'Well, what are we going to play? What *are* we going to do, boys? I don't know any of these things you play.' And he looked down and saw our stock arrangements we had open and were playing. And he took the violin bow and turned two or three of them over—and he saw one.

"It was 'Number 69.' Benny asked, 'What is *that?* That looks easy.' Callihan, our director, said, 'That's 'Love In Bloom.' So Benny took the fiddle and tuned it a little bit, then turned around to everybody and says, 'I'm gonna play this one. It's Number Sixty-Nine. That's Love In Bloom! Boys, get out Sixty-Nine!' One of the special guests shouted, 'THAT'S NOT A NUMBER! *THAT'S A GAME!*' Everybody laughed. Hell, I didn't even know what he was talkin' about.

"Anyway, Jack played that tune, and he played it so horribly that he stopped the show. That was the beginning, and I think it was the first time he did Love In Bloom (the ditty that Jack Benny used from then on for his theme song on radio and TV).

Graham Crackers also accommodated guest performers, such as Ben Bernie, who was featured on the Blue Ribbon Malt Show with the Columbia Broadcasting Network. When Ben wanted to take a vacation in Miami from his gig at the Hotel Sherman in Chicago, he fulfilled his broadcast contract by using Graham's orchestra, and at this time, Ned started noticing that broadcasting had much to do with where the band was placed.

The Crackers played for one week at the Casa de Baile (Home of Dance) in Jacksonville, Florida, then played a second week for a giant General Motors' show. The bandstand was in the middle of all the cars and, as Ned saw it, the band was the main attraction.

On the last night of the show the bass player made friends with some ladies and cooked up a date. He and Ned took out *three* raving beauties in a big Buick. They took along a gallon jar of Greek wine (their version of the "Noble Experiment") and motored out of town to a place called Hyde Park—out in the woods—where the girls introduced them to the local Lover's Lane.

They pulled the shades down all the way around the Buick, and were poised for a little wine tasting, or whatever fun they might get into, when **POW!**—a pistol shot rang off next to the left front window of their sedan! A man jumped on the running board, and when Ned pulled back the shade to peek out, the intruder pointed a gun in his face and screamed, "GIT OUTTA THIS CAR AND PUT YOUR HANDS IN THE AIR!" The guys and dolls were absolutely petrified as three land pirates ripped opened the doors to search and rob them. One guy jammed his gun into Ned's ribs, but missed the three dollars in his vest pocket (where the gun was pressed). Ned was chuckling to himself until they took one girl's ring off and she cried, "That's my wedding ring! Don't take *that!*" (At this moment the boys in the band first realized that at least one of their dates was "hitched!") The pirates took everything else, ripped out all the wires on the headlights, and made their departure with the warning, *"If you follow us, we'll kill ya!"* There would be no "Love In Bloom" in Hyde Park that night. It took them twenty minutes to figure out the wires on the headlights to get back to their hotel, and reporting the robbery was out of the question. Two of their dates were married to guys who would come after them.

With a sigh of relief, they left Jacksonville the next day for Savannah and five fun-filled summer weeks on Tybee Island—where there were gobs of girls who always wanted to meet visiting bandsmen. They played on a beachfront pavilion each night, rehearsed three times each week, then were free to sprawl on the beach.

The owner's wife was Thelma Terry. She was a famous bass-playing bandleader in the late 1920's. Her specialty was playing an abnormally large bass banjo that stood taller than herself, and had to be supported with a special stand. Because of Thelma, musicians were highly regarded on Tybee Island. She was instrumental in bringing Cab Calloway down to Savannah for one weekend from the Cotton Club in New York's Harlem. Cab was a terrific person whom Ned enjoyed, and it was the first time Ned attended a party where whites mingled freely with blacks. (This was a big change from Ned's State of West Virginia in 1932.)

Broadcasting was "king," but they did few "remotes." MCA, for instance, sent the Graham Crackers to Pittsburgh just before Labor Day to work The Willows, a large outdoor-indoor patio combination where two bands were featured. They did their broadcasting from nearby WWS. In Charleston, South Carolina, they went once each week through fifteen miles of swamp to get to the radio station at the Francis Marion Hotel (named after General Francis Marion, the "Swamp Fox," who was so elusive to the English during the American Revolution). At Savannah, they drove to Victory Drive, traveling fifteen miles to broadcast from the Hotel DeSoto. MCA generally booked them near a broadcast facility, but another agency got them off the beaten track to fill a cancellation by the Isham Jones Orchestra—a leading name in the 1930's. Where Isham went is a question, but they went in his stead to play in Salisbury, Maryland for a large community dance held smack in the middle of town. Everyone expected Isham Jones, but nobody there had ever seen him. Upon discovering there was no Isham, they nearly ran the band out of town. The folks were really hacked about it, but that didn't bother the band too much. It was a reliable booking agency that worked through the Union, and they knew they'd be paid.

Extracting themselves from Salisbury, they headed up to Martinsville, Virginia to play on a Blue Ridge Mountain top, after which they were stuck in a little town for a three day layover. There was little for them to do there except hang out in the main lobby of their hotel and listen to the radio, or do some reading (not what *these* boys were accustomed to). Restless, Ned and a few other musicians decided to take a stroll. They no sooner walked out the front doors when they heard a revival meeting going on across the street in a large brick church. This had apparently been going on for one full week. It was hot out, and the windows were wide open so they could look in and see the evangelist—a fire and brimstone type preacher going at it with a vengeance. The church was packed.

The following day the boys were sitting around the lobby when in walks that evangelist. He had a room there. The lead trumpet player from Columbia, Pennsylvania—who was a little older—was starting to "tie one on." He drummed up a poker game, and herded everybody up to one of the rooms to get going on it.

They pulled up some chairs around a bed, and the trumpet man had dealt a few hands of five-card stud when there was a knock on the door. He told Ned, "Git that goddamn door, will ya?" Ned obliged and, lo and behold, it was the preacher.

He says, "You boys mind if I come in? I overheard you were going to have a game. I've nothin' to do."

Ned said, "Sure, come on in."

No sooner did he get through the door than the trumpeter disdainfully tossed the deck of cards on the bed. Leaning way back in his chair, and twirling his finger in his highball, he accusingly said, "You're the *preacher!* We been watchin' you downstairs 'n' across the street. How come you (hic) don't—"

"Well, that's my job doin' that," retorted the preacher. "I don't mind 'n' it don't hurt to have a little recreation."

Boy oh boy, thought Ned. *Here's an evangelist preacher, like that! And all those big crowds? And stayin' here at this hotel, and coming and getting in a poker game with a bunch of jazz musicians?*

As it turned out, "Preacher Man" was a card shark. "Trumpet Man" caught on to it and they started to fight! Cass Sanders (the banjo player who was, more or less, one of the older guys—a kind of straw boss) tried to calm down the trumpeter as Ned hung on to one of his arms. As they were doing this, the "holy one" up and grabs all the money and splits. Ned saw him take the money and run out the door. Raised a Presbyterian, Ned asked himself, *If evangelism is show business, what are they doing it in a church for?* He couldn't get this phony out of his mind for some time.

Ned later received a telephone call from Jack Evans, with whom he had worked as both a Wildcat and a Cracker. Jack convinced Ned to come down to Carolina in September and join him in Jack Baxter's band—a Hal Kemp style band with an exceptionally good sax section. Johnny Best, one of the finest trumpet players that Ned had run across, was also in the band. They worked eleven cotillions for VIP cadets out of the Virginia Polytechnic Institute.

Ned roomed with Jack, and they started hanging out together. When Thanksgiving Day rolled around, Jack invited Ned to dinner at his mother's house in Greensboro, North Carolina, a two or three hour drive away. There, Ned met Jack's sister, Gladys. Her father was a medical doctor, but *she* played piano! Her other brother, Clinton, played tuba with Paul Whiteman and John Phillip Sousa. He was recorded, and was beginning to play the Ringling Brothers and the Barnum and Bailey circuits, gigs that would keep him busy for the next thirty-four years. They all had plenty to talk about, and had a good ol' time.

When the holiday gigs ended, Jack invited Ned to dinner again, and also invited Fats Parish, the bass player who owned a "machine" and could motor them there and back. On the return trip, Ned suddenly roared, "STOP THE CAR!"

"What d'ya mean 'stop'? We're halfway there!" complained Fats.

"Because I have found her," purred Ned, "and I have to go back and see Gladys."

Within two days, Ned Guthrie courted, proposed to, and married Gladys Virginia Evans, arranging their ceremony to be held in Charleston, West Virginia in the same house he had seen his parents wed the second time around. There was no waiting period there in 1933, and "money was no object." (He had all of forty dollars and Gladys had ten.) Together, they would face tough times on the road—but Gladys, for her part, was no wimp. Years later, for instance, when Gladys was *sixty-four* years old, she and Ned found themselves in an extremly dangerous situation when they were with friends in New Orleans taking a short vacation. "Fats" Gonzales was driving, Ned was in the right front seat, and Gladys was sitting directly behind him next to Fats's wife and daughter in the back. They apparently had been watched, because immediately upon pulling up into their usual parking space, two professional robbers, backed up with a driver in a getaway car, came up on either side of them. One of them *put a knife to Ned's throat!* Another one grabbed the child out of the car, and held a knife to *her* throat! This triggered the "ultimate warrior" in Gladys. She grabbed a throw pillow with her right hand, and jammed it between the knife and Ned's neck. Glancing down, she spotted her gripsack, snatched it up, and

NED AND GLADYS IN BALTIMORE 1935

began vigorously beating the assailant in the face. Nonstop splattering sounds of rapid-fire slaps, whacks, and some thuds were interspersed with her screaming "DON'T CUT MY HUSBAND!" She caught them by surprise. They scattered, but Ned jumped out of the car, leapt at his bloodied assailant, and grabbed onto his leg. The robber got away only after dragging Ned for ten yards or so, and in this push and pull struggle, Ned suffered knife cuts on the wrist and banged both of his knees, injuring one of them badly. It could have been worse. Gladys had saved the day.

After their wedding, Ned continued working and traveling with top-notch musicians. Johnny Best, for one, would later play in Benny Goodman's band and with Bob Crosby and the Bobcats. He later also traveled with Glenn Miller to Europe.

Ned had become good friends with Johnny in Jack Baxter's Orchestra, but they got separated in Washington, D.C. when Ned formed a band with Hugh Alexander, a banjo player with some connections. They brought in tenor saxophone player Paul Wingate and Ross Pierson on alto sax. Jack Evans was the trombonist, and Wayland Redden was on trumpet. It was a dynamite band, but Ned and Hugh had problems keeping it working. They ended up splitting it into two ensembles—one band working the San Remo Restaurant, and the other one placed at the Old Hickory.

There at the Old Hickory, Ned met a disc jockey who played banjo and guitar. He wanted to sit in, but Ned and some of the other musicians wouldn't let him. According to Ned, "Arthur Godfrey played a jazzy-style, four-string guitar like you would play a ukulele. Dance musicians wanted another beat."

Later, most of these band members again joined Jan Campbell's Orchestra. In New York, ASC had them play under the name of "Ben Barton and his Californians" for stage presentations. The music was as "square" as "Git Along Little

Doggie" could be, and Ben Barton told Jan Campbell that he wasn't going to have some bald saxophonist kneeling at a campfire in his opening act. (The shine on Ned's dome had been improving since he was seventeen years old.) He laughs about it now, but prior to Ben's shows, Ned could be found backstage—applying shoe polish to his bald head to keep Ben on an even keel.

Before Ned's head had taken on a permanent cordovan glow, Campbell's band was sent on tour throughout New England and New York State. They played in Salem at Northshore Gardens and the Copley Square Hotel in Boston.

After one-night stands at Lake Winnipesaukee and Manchester in New Hampshire, they headed out for Lake Champlain at Burlington, Vermont. On the way up there, Homer Curtis was at the wheel. Homer played banjo very well. He did all of Eddy Peabody's tunes, and also performed special arrangements of his original material. "He sure couldn't drive a car too well, though," Ned countered. Homer drove through the downtown section of Concord, New Hampshire, and whizzed past the governor's car blasting his horn. The state police had trouble digesting that, so they called ahead.

Just before one leaves New Hampshire, there is a place called Caanon. Homer came to a skidding stop in front of this town's one and only (hand-crank) gas pump. The attendant gave them the word that the cops had called, and told them to stay put until they got there.

"So we took off," says Guthrie. "And we were just about to cross—I think it was the Connecticut River—to get to Vermont. And the road was winding and rolling. And, we approached a one-way culvert over a creek in a big farm field. And standing there was a cop. And he was a country cop. And he had been plowing. And only one car could get over the bridge. *And* he had a shotgun. And he pointed it at us!

"He arrested us and took us back to the state police. We didn't have bail, so Jack Hollingsworth left a real good wristwatch there for bail. We got across that bridge into the other state, then sped off to Lake Champlain. That was truly a dumb thing."

They broadcast on WGY in Schenectady, New York—a 50,000 watt station boosted to 500,000 watts—to broadcast experimental short waves to Brazil. WGY was owned by General Electric, and Jan Campbell's band was chosen by GE to represent American jazz music for a series of five weekly broadcasts.

Their next gig was for five weeks at Lake Owasco in Auburn, New York. Most bands that played Owasco for any length of time ended up entertaining inmates at the Auburn State Prison. Ned played in the women's section where he remembers serenading a high-profile stickup lady known nationally as the "Blonde Bandit."

While working in Auburn, which is twenty or thirty miles west of Syracuse in the western part of the state, Campbell had them traveling all the way to Boston to play on Mondays for the Battle of the Bands Night. Armed with some good jazz arrangements, matching grey suits, and their stage show, Jan Campbell's band won hands-down for three weeks. They were confident and rightly so, but the last band to compete was Stan Stanley's from Northern Ohio. Stan was bald as a cue ball. Ned thought, *Man, that's how I'm going to look!*

It was a musicians' band without the entertainment, but they played jazz—and played it well. They also had a trumpet player who came down front and sang through a megaphone. "And boy oh boy," reflects Ned, "we thought we had a good vocalist in Benny Griffen, who was doing Armstrong-like deals and acting crazy. But *this fellow,* with his wavy hair— every time he sang, he stopped them from dancing, and they'd gather 'round when he was doing his tunes. And that very night I heard the booker from Boston—he sat there during intermission—offer him a job to come with him and let him put a band around him. That's the way Vaughn Monroe got his start."

It wasn't the best of situations for families on the road, although several bandsmen, whether by design or necessity, had wives and children with them. They were always on the move. In Washington, D.C., Ned rehearsed a band that Jan Campbell took over and got working at the Villa Roma, and later traveled the coal fields of Pennsylvania. They stayed in Harrisburg and drove seventy-five miles on Tuesdays, Thursdays, and Saturdays to broadcast over WCAU from the Chez Vous Ballroom in Philadelphia. A new lead trumpet player— a powerhouse—joined the band in Harrisburg, but he went on a liquor toot and split up with his wife, and drifted off somewhere. The band needed a replacement, and Gladys was off visiting her mother. When the band was ready to head out for New York City to play shows for Ben Barton (the anti-bald head guy), Ned decided to kill two birds with one stone.

Ned and Sticks Hartman, the bass player, borrowed a roadster and drove down to Greensboro, North Carolina. Before scooping up Gladys, they went to the place where Ned knew Johnny Best was playing trumpet with the Tal Henry Band. They were bunked-out over a bowling alley, so Ned quietly crept up the stairs and found Johnny asleep on an army cot, woke him up, and sold him on coming to where people could hear him. "It's not like you have a percentage of anything here," Ned reminded him. "You don't *have* anything!"

They picked up Gladys. She rode in the front of the roadster with the driver, Sticks, while Ned and John yakked all the way to New York in the rumble seat through the snow.

Under Ben Barton's baton in New York they mostly did stage reviews—like at the Majestic Theatre in Jersey City and a large vaudeville house in Patterson. They also worked for two weeks at the Mount Morris Theatre in Harlem on Lennox Avenue. They were doing reasonably well (considering the depression), but one week went without food. The Chesterfield Hotel, where they were staying, didn't have a dining room. They couldn't run a tab. Some of the musicians had gone to the theatre manager to ask for an advance, pointing out that many of them had their families with them. The manager gave them an unbending "NO!" There was some strike-talk, then Ned had a brainstorm.

It was Wednesday, and the band's payday fell on Fridays—two long, lean days away. They were all hungry. Ned called Gladys, and told her to grab a train and come uptown, saying, "WE'RE GONNA EAT!" She had only five pennies that Ned had left her (enough for a one-way fare), so she ducked under the turnstile. By the time she arrived, Ned had gathered all twenty-seven of them together—then marched them into a Waldorf Restaurant to "mash down" a hot meal.

All in the timing, when the magic moment arrived to pay the bills, Guthrie scooped them up and told the cashier, "We're with Ben Barton and his Californians over in the show at the Mount Morris. I'll sign these 'n' pick 'em up tomorrow."

"Sure," said the cashier, "wait right here." Then he went out and grabbed two of "New York's Finest," who just happened to be out front. They entered the scene, and were ready to call the paddy wagon when Ned made his move.

"Well look officer, we're not trying to do anything wrong. We're working at the Mount Morris Theatre in the orchestra."

"So what!" said the cop, eyeing him suspiciously.

"I'll tell you what," advanced Ned (pointing to Gladys, who feigned a smile), "you keep her. That's my wife. You let me go over to see the manager, because we have money coming over there. And I'll get him to do it. It's not like we're sneaking out of here. We want to pay!"

"Is he over there for sure?" asked one cop.

"Yes! He's over there," Ned assured him.

"How you know you're gonna get it?" questioned the other cop.

"Because if he doesn't pay he won't have a show" replied Ned. "He's got people over there he's already sold tickets to. They're waiting for the movie part to get off and the stage show to come on."

So Ned and "the law" went to the office of the Mount Morris Theatre where Ned made his spiel to the manager.

"These god-*damn* musicians! We're not going to have *any* show!" was the manager's response.

Ned insisted, "We're hungry and we have to *eat!* Well, it's up to you. You just pay this bill or you don't have any show. *Now what are you going to do?*"

The manager was livid, but coughed up the money, cussing all the while he did it.

They finished their run at the Mount Morris that Friday night. During the final performance, a big iron pipe used for ballast on the theatre curtain fell down with a terrific crash, penetrating the wooden floor of the stage—right between Johnny Best and Ned Guthrie—who both kept playing as though nothing had happened. That pipe was still sticking up between them when the curtain came down. In addition to his feeling that his "Man" had been with him again, Ned became convinced, as the years went by, that somebody had been trying to get even with him.

Ned and Gladys returned to Charleston from New York, and Ned landed a job working for fellow named Art Bolts. His band, "Art Bolts and his Nuts," worked a dance marathon.

Contestants danced and the Nuts played for fifty minutes, then they all rested for ten minutes. There was a master of ceremonies, a lot of singing and joke-cracking, and the whole thing was how long it could go. This one lasted for nine weeks.

After that gig, Ned decided to treat Gladys and himself to a rare day off. They went to take a romantic excursion on the *Washington,* an Ohio and Mississippi River boat out of St. Louis, Missouri. It was the second largest steamer of its kind—with six decks and a brig, with a large barge of coal in tow at its side. By law, the crew of eighty men were all seamen in the U.S. Merchant Marine. Patrons paid three dollars for a six hour excursion, and most of them fed the one-armed bandits. The *Washington* traveled the Ohio River, stopping at towns from Paducah, Kentucky to Pittsburgh, Pennsylvania, and back. Ned and Gladys were relaxing, getting ready to live it up, when the band took a break. One of the musicians came sauntering by, and Ned said hello. He ended up talking with him, and the guy mentioned that the sax player had a family emergency, and needed to leave the band as soon as they could find a replacement.

"No shit!" exclaimed Ned. "I play alto, clarinet, and baritone. I've got 'em out in the car back on the levee."

Ned sat in, was hired—and so went their romantic steamboat ride. Gladys was disappointed, but knew that they needed the money, so she disembarked to visit her mother again.

Musicians were categorized as seamen, and received good pay with four solid meals thrown in each day. The only annoyance was competing with the "cheu-shay, cheu-shay" of the steamer's smokestack, not to mention the calliope that ballyhooed away as they tried to tune-up the band. Evening excursions were called "moonlights" and sometimes were caught in fog. Returning to dock in thick fog was dangerous and slow as they marked the twain, edging this huge flatbottom steamer that was often overladen with customers towards shore. The band played all night, if necessary, to keep the patrons happy.

When this gig ended, Ned disembarked at Paducah, Kentucky, took the train home to Charleston, and picked up Gladys. He found some work in speakeasies in West Virginia, then joined Floyd Mills and his Marylanders in Wilmington, Delaware. They worked the Old Heidelberg, and then went on to Philadelphia to work a location job at the famous club called The Rafters. They also worked the Philco Radio and Television Club. It featured bands on two of its three floors. In 1934, all these clubs were large and widely known establishments with remote radio broadcasting facilities.

Late one winter night in Philadelphia, after a Saturday night theatre job in Bridgeston, New Jersey, Ned and the rest of the players in Jack Griffith's Columbia Broadcasting Orchestra drove sixty-three miles to cram in an extra appearance at the Philco Radio and Television Club. They pulled up and hurriedly unpacked. Ned, struggling with three horns and a fat band book, was the last one to head up a short set of stairs to the door with the little window. At the head of those stairs was a large policeman who had on a blue greatcoat with buttons down to his knees.

"You want me to give you a hand?" he asked.

"Yeah, sure officer," replied Ned.

"You want me to open the door, Sir?" asked the officer.

Ned answered, "Good. Thank you, officer!"

He opened the door for Ned and then asked, "You want to step in?"

Ned thought, *My God, this guy's polite. What's the matter with him?*

As he stepped inside the club he saw all kinds of people

standing around—musicians, customers, and cops galore. The officer who "helped" Ned shouted, "OKAY! THAT'S ALL OF 'EM! CALL THE WAGONS!"

This happened in North Philadelphia because of its "blue law" that forbade clubs to operate past midnight on Saturday night. Ned had walked up those stairs at twenty minutes after the bewitching hour.

The Westmorland Police Precinct was located on the same block as the club that got busted, but they didn't walk anybody around the corner to the station. Instead, everybody had to board the paddy wagons that pulled up shortly with screeching fanfare. The musicians were the last people herded into the wagons.

They arrived at the place of incarceration and were put into an enclosed breezeway between two buildings. One hundred and seventy-three people, in all, had to be booked and assigned cells. There was one door with two long lines slowly going in and coming out. Ned looked over and spotted the guitar player in the line coming out of the booking sergeant's room. All the musicians were supposed to be last, but here he was in the opposite line—already processed—and standing one yard away. Curious as to what was up ahead, Ned took a step in that direction to speak with him. A big, burly guard saw Ned out of line and bellowed, "GIT' BACK IN THAT LINE YOU SONOFABITCH!" Then he gave Ned a shove—into the wrong line! There would have been about one hundred people in front of Ned had he done anything but smile at the guitar player, who muffled a giggle. Ned spent the night in jail but wasn't booked. They never got his name.

There were two tiers of cages. On top, there were six cells with women packed into them like sardines. The men were caged on the bottom floor. When Ned entered his cell, it was occupied by an old man, a dirty toilet, and a small bench. He and the guitarist sat on the bench and began telling jokes. Within minutes there were twenty-eight "toasted," if not "plastered," men crowded into that cell that was meant to accommodate no more than six or eight prisoners.

Ned left his baritone sax and other things at the Philco Club—everything but his alto sax. Everybody was standing back-to-back, and there was no way anyone could sit down *with the exception of the two musicians on the bench.* Sometime around four-thirty in the wee morning, the guys began to sober up. They were all tired and crabby. One fellow remarked, "Those goddamn musicians sittin' over there all night long. They're not doin' anything! So why don't they get out their horns and *play* something?"

Ned hollered over to him, "We can't play in here!" but some guy grabbed him and another one got his hands on the guitar player. They quickly "unholstered their weapons" and shot off a ditty. Everybody in that jail knew the big hit "The Object Of My Affection" (has turned my complexion, from white to rosy red). These Philadelphians in their "City of Brotherly Love" thought that it was ridiculous that they were arrested in a club, so they had the musicians play The Object Of My Affection—and they sang it and sang it. The musicians kept playing it over and over and over. The jailers, as might be expected, got more and more aggravated, so they threw buckets of water on them several times to make them quit. This marathon sing-out, however, ended when it was time to face the judge. He came out on Sunday morning, and released everybody on their own recognizance, because the Philco people went to bat for their customers.

Ned got on the subway and rode down to Broad Street, then changed lines and went out to 51st Street to where he was living with Gladys. He had picked up the morning paper, and on the front page the headline read, "DANCE MUSIC PLAYED

IN CELL BY ORCHESTRA." He carried that clipping around for years—for luck.

An alto sax player named Pete Shafer talked Ned into staying in Philadelphia, and began taking him to the musicians' union hall every Wednesday and Friday. The Philadelphia Local owned its own building on 18th Street, and the hiring hall accommodated up to two hundred musicians. This started Ned booking gigs on a weekly basis. There was a podium that rested about six feet up from the floor—above everybody. A union officer had a microphone to make announcements, page people, and list gigs. Two sections were on a diagonal, with the Italians musicians in one corner, and the Jewish musicians in the opposite corner. There was no in-between. A musician either worked with one group or the other. This is where musicians picked up their weekend gigs.

Ned had decided to stay in this town because of the Columbia Broadcasting Orchestra. It was a twelve-piece band that did many shows every month, but never on Sundays. Jewish parties, however, were held on Sundays. A Jewish drummer named Jack Shapiro, who had worked with Ned in the State Ballroom at Columbia Square, liked Ned's playing. He needed a good clarinet man, and offered to teach Ned the music. Jewish music challenged Ned's skill, but he bought all the available books and practiced.

Ned was with Floyd Mills and his Marylanders in the early summer of 1935, working the Mayfair Gardens in Baltimore. He got a night off when Louis Armstrong was scheduled to appear, so he moonlighted as a waiter. He had never been that "hung-up" about "Satchmo"—not compared to "Red Nichols and his Five Pennies"—but he was curious and wanted to see him in person.

After Satchmo's first strenuous set, Ned realized what everybody was talking about. While the band was still playing, Satchmo took a short break and left the bandstand. It was a long way from the bar area to the bandstand, but Ned saw him go backstage and followed him.

There was Louis in a razzy-dazzy aqua blue uniform with fancy cuffs 'n' collar and patent leather shoes. Absolutely drenched in sweat, he stood with a large pitcher of ice water and an oversize handkerchief in one hand—trumpet tucked under his arm—wiping the sweat off his face, and smoking. He smiled at Ned and commented, "I'm jus' havin' a little ice tea. I's gots to have my ice tea." Then he laughed and repeated, "I's *gots* ta have my ice tea!" They joked and chatted for four or five minutes. Ned told him that he played in the house band, "but I sure admire you and your band." Later Guthrie stated, "He was real nice to me, and that was the first time I had someone of such greatness all to myself. And he was straight—right from the heart in everything he said."

When the Marylanders left Baltimore for Buckroe Beach on Chesapeake Bay in Virginia, Gladys thought that at last she was pregnant. Ned sent her to Greensboro so she could see her family doctor, and later met her in Hampton, Virginia. Sure enough, she was! Cooing, Ned remembers, "I will never forget that beautiful woman in that orchid knit dress when she got off the bus. She was really something for me to quit the road for." Ned told her, "Hell, I'm not going to drag you through acres and high waters, so we're going back to West Virginia to raise a family."

He wasn't sure how he was going to support a family by working out of one town as a local musician, but he'd been traveling for eight years, and had never liked seeing kids on the road. They boarded the C&O Railroad on a three dollar excursion ticket, and returned home to Charleston.

When they arrived, a telegram came in from Floyd Mills, offering Ned an opportunity to travel to Europe on the new

French luxury liner, the *Normandie*. Tempted by this opportunity, Ned asked if they'd take wives. When they said "No," he replied "Forget it!"

Ned landed a WPA job with the United States Treasury Department in Charleston working a check-writing machine that paid all the WPA projects in West Virginia and western Virginia. That brought home twenty-five dollars and twenty-five cents per week. There was no chance of a promotion, but he would stay on that job for five years. He couldn't live on that salary, but directly across from where he worked on Summers Street was a bar in a basement. Ned knew it would be a good place to play music and, six months after Ned had returned to Charleston, a job opened at the Rathskeller (one week after Ned Guthrie, Jr. was born on February 20th of 1936). As a bandleader, Ned would earn eighteen dollars each week. On that, and his day gig—plus some additional income from teaching private music lessons—Ned was doing alright for a musician in Charleston, West Virginia in the mid-1930's.

CHARLESTONIANS
Top: Glenna Thompson, Ned Guthrie, Bob Lamm, Willys Scott
Photograph by Robert W. McKinnon
Bottom: June Wolfe, Howell Brown, Ned Guthrie,
Steve Cannon, Dick Fultz
Photographer Unknown

Street of Dreams

The Rathskeller was located under the Lincoln Hotel. Up on Summers Street, you could hear the band's wail through the steel grating in the sidewalk. When a fight broke out between two or three people, within minutes there would be a hundred people scuffling and police trying to get through. Up and down Summers Street it would be the same thing.[2]

Once in the "sanctuary" of the nightclub, only occasional fisticuffs would erupt. The club's beer license was at stake, so when a fight broke out, Ned and the drummer, Steve Kaman, would hurriedly "hang up their axes" long enough to jump off the stage out into the war zone. Ned would grab one guy and the drummer would grab the other one, then they'd hustle them out of the bar—out of sight, out of mind, good riddance! It got hectic sometimes, but people flooded into the Rathskeller every night as the band played on.

The Rathskeller became a way of life. From colorful "ladies of the night" working the street above, to preachers, country club people, and state house figures—a full spectrum of Charlestonians and out-of-towners were lured into this cellar by the potent combination of wine, women, and song.[3]

Star performers and "class acts" that worked the Middleburg Auditorium further spiced the scene with impromptu performances. Almost every band that came through Charleston spent Sunday and Monday nights jamming with Ned's combo, "The Charlestonians"—bands like Ben Bernie, Little Jack Little, Woody Herman, Harry James, and others. On one high occasion when Artie Shaw's band hit town, Ned's friend, Johnny Best, who was with Artie's band, brought "Lady Day" down into the Rathskeller on her break.[4] (Ned had a system worked out with cabbies who shuttled performers through crosstown traffic from their showplace to the Rathskeller and back again, within the timespan of the performer's usual break of thirty minutes.) Racial prejudices and standards of conduct that musicians then observed in the South were brushed aside as Ned glowingly introduced this extraordinary woman. She sang a ballad called "Bill," then went into a blues. At the Rathskeller, Billie Holiday made them all stand up and scream.

The U.S. Army was drafting most every trumpet player in the country in the late 1930's. Sometime in 1939, Ned had lost all of his trumpet players to the military, and was hard-pressed to find one good player. A friend named Robert Armstrong, who was with Henry Busse's Orchestra, suggested he get in touch with Bob Lamm in Newcastle, Pennsylvania. Armstrong told Guthrie, "He plays like Satchmo and Bobby Hackett, all rolled into one."

"You've got to be kidding!" exclaimed Ned.

"There's one problem," warned Armstrong. "You might not want him. He's blind."

"No, I don't want him," Ned replied. "People come to hear

the band. They have enough problems. They don't want to sit out there and feel sorry for someone."

Armstrong told him, "You get in touch with him anyway. Give 'im a call."

Ned couldn't help harboring the thought that a blind man onstage would "bum out" his patrons. He was up front about that. Lamm told him, "You can't tell I'm blind by looking at me, and I don't use a cane or a Seeing Eye dog. If you let me come down for two weeks, I'll pay my own way. If I'm not satisfactory, I'll come back."

As Bob Lamm's evening "on the spit" approached, his public audition became the subject of gossip that traveled up and down Summers—the street that had become known as "the street of dreams."

Ned picked up Bob, his wife, and his boy at the old K&M train depot the night before his Charleston debut, and put them up at the Park Hotel. By the time Bob lifted his trumpet to his lips for that first note, the Rathskeller was wall-to-wall with bodies—everyone wanting to know if Ned Guthrie would hire the blind man, or run him off! No doubt, bets were placed.

On the bandstand, Ned asked Bob what he wanted to open with, but Bob answered, "You call it." After Bob played the first tune everybody was grinning and applauding him— knowing he had the gig—because he "tore it up." On another occasion, Harry James's piano man and his saxophonist sat in while Harry and Helen Forest relaxed and listened at a table. They watched and marveled at how Bob played a jazz version of the waltz "Charmaine." Harry James later recorded it with his entire trumpet section playing what Bob had played that night at the Rathskeller.

Guthrie was impressed with Bob's command of his horn and his lyrical style of improvising. Perhaps "lyric" was the key word. For reasons, Guthrie got it in his head that Bob should sing. Not one to keep such thoughts to himself—and a bandleader who ran a "tight ship"—Ned was on Bob's case.

"You ought to try singing," said Guthrie.

"I never sang," Bob replied.

"It's easy," prompted Ned. "Anybody can sing a blues."

"Naw, I don't think so," said the reluctant Lamm.

Ned tried, "I'll tell you the words."

Bob was shaking his bowed head, mumbling, "No, no—"

Ned pulled rank on him saying, "The trumpet players always sing in our band. It's *always* been like that. When I get a five dollar tip, all you've got to do is stand there and sing. I'll whisper ahead of each phrase and tell you the words. Nobody will see or hear me."

"But I don't sing!" pleaded Bob.

Ned insisted, "Oh yes you do sing, too!"

At this juncture, Ned spotted a man who always tipped the band five bucks if they played his wife's favorite tune, "When Did You Leave Heaven." He was accustomed to hearing his request sung.

Ned commanded Bob, "You're going to sing the next tune!"

"I don't sing!" cried Bob—as Ned shoved the microphone into his hand, and counted off the request.

As it turned out, Bob Lamm emerged a natural born singer—destined for success.

The Charlestonians had packed the place every night they performed for over six years. Given a little help from wine and women, the Rathskeller was a total success.

Nevertheless, this artistic blues and jazz haven where traveling celebrities performed for free, dancers danced, and so-called high- and lowbrows brushed shoulders together at an oasis—all this life proved to be as fragile as could be. One day a vendor with a new contraption made an offer the owner couldn't refuse. "Why pay this band ninety dollars a week," the vendor reasoned, "when you can put in a jukebox and pocket sixty or seventy bucks a week?"

He might as well have lobbed a grenade into the band room—**BAM!** The Charlestonians were put on notice, and soon the vendor's delivery boy glibly rolled in "the box." And that was that—the end of an era—this bar in a basement.

Ned took his Charlestonians into an after-hours club called the Gypsy Village. They already had a jukebox. Ned eyed it suspiciously, and began competing with it—cutting breaks short, putting the tips bucket on his head, and playing clarinet to get attention (something the jukebox couldn't do). The other musicians would join in and get louder than the jukebox, then Ned would signal the waitress to *pull the plug!*[5]

Bob Lamm was still in the band when they did floor shows at the Gypsy Village. Since the shows carried their own directors, Ned became Bob's Seeing Eye. He'd sit on the right side of Bob and give him foot signals, directing starts and stops by either pressing his foot on top of Bob's shoe, or bumping the side of it. How a blind man could catch the director's cues was the talk of the town.

Things went so well at the Gypsy Village that the Rathskeller began losing business. Its owners wanted Ned back, but the Charlestonians played Gypsy's for two and one-half years. One owner was a gambler interested in one of the show singers, and kept her on after her show ended to work with the band. She was a "looker" but not a full-fledged vocalist, and soon ran out of material. The owner started getting on Guthrie's case.

"She doesn't have any music to play!" Ned told him.

"Well," retorted the owner, "you'll play whatever she wants. You'll do it, or you won't work!"

Ned stewed about that all night. When he got home, he telephoned Francis Craig in Nashville and got him out of bed.

Craig was a rich gentleman, and as to awakening him, Ned commented, "You don't *do that,* but *I* did."

Ned told him, "Wayland Redden is in your band and he tried to get me to come down there about six months ago. Is the job still open? I'll double on baritone sax."

Craig replied, "Why yes, yes—but why are you calling me at two-thirty in the morning?"

"Because," answered Ned, "tomorrow I might change my mind."

"Well, if you play like Wayland says you do, you've got the job."

"There's just one thing though," added Ned, "I've got a blind trumpet player who is a very good singer—Bob Lamm. You just lost Snooky Lanson and you don't have a vocalist. Bob can really do it!"

Craig hesitated. "Well, I don't know about that!"

"I'll make a recording for you, if you want me to," Ned offered.

Craig thought for a moment, then made an offer to pay Ned union scale and transportation saying, "And we'll see?"

Guthrie made a 78 RPM acetate disc of Lamm singing "It Had To Be You," accompanied by guitarist Billy Williams with himself on clarinet. When Craig heard it, he hired both Ned and Bob. Ned gave notice at the Gypsy Village, and handed his band over to Darell Blair. Then the Lamms and Guthries (including Diane Virginia Guthrie, born in November of 1941) headed out for Nashville, Tennessee in a high frame of mind.

Francis Craig's orchestra had been featured at the Hermitage Hotel since 1928. His wife—whom Ned characterizes as a lovely lady of her own means and fortune—had bought the hotel, as Nashville rumor had it, to keep her husband off the road. The dining and ballrooms had fifty thousand dollars worth of gold leaf on the ceiling. On the walls leading into the cellar lounge were slabs of pure onyx. The customers were Southern blue bloods, and there was no dancing—just elegant dining, potables, and listening.

Craig's orchestra had toured the universities—playing proms and fraternity dances throughout Alabama, Mississippi, and Kentucky. When he developed tuberculosis in the 1930's, Craig and the band's families moved lock, stock, and barrel out to Denver, Colorado. For several years, "Francis Craig's Serenade" was aired by NBC on Sunday evenings to the nation. When his health improved, they all moved back to Nashville. So they say, that's when Mrs. Craig made her move and bought the hotel, and went into the broadcasting business. In the 1920's, the Craig family insurance business had already established Radio Station WSM (We Shield Millions, the Air Castle of the South). It was picked up by NBC, a one hundred and fifty-five station network.

When Ned laid eyes on Craig's bandbook, he was astonished to see that his third sax chair had once been held by James Melton, a Metropolitan Opera tenor. Ned later met him in a nightclub in Philadelphia, and learned that Dinah Shore had sung with Craig's band over WSM in her teens—when her name was still "Fanny Rose." Phil Harris, who later married Alice Faye, played drums with Craig, and an Armenian woman named Kay Armen broadcasted and did army shows, along with Kitty Kalen. Bob Lamm replaced Snooky Lanson, and Ned replaced Cecil Bailey on baritone sax, an instrument that was particularly hard to replace during World War II. Bailey went into the service in 1942, so Craig needed baritone sax for a rhythmical bass line introduction in his theme song, "Red Rose." Pianist and arranger Owen Bradley had written special arrangements to stuff three band books. It was a luxurious library, particularly in those days.

Ned's "funky" style of improvising and his baritone playing

attracted the attention of another orchestra leader who hired him to moonlight with WSIX, a mutual broadcasting station. Craig wanted to have the exclusive sound of baritone sax on the airways, so he broached this subject with Ned.

"Well, can you replace this money?" Ned immediately asked him. At this, Craig coughed up what Ned terms "a moderate raise" and Ned stopped working for the competition.

Nashville was the center of the army training for D-Day. There were twenty-three counties in Tennessee used for maneuvers. Every place you looked it was army. Craig's Orchestra played for a number of USO-type canteen shows, and Grand Old Opry stars, such as Minnie Pearl and Whitey Ford, the "Duke of Paducah" were regulars.

There was also a struggling young guy Craig used who was billed as the "Tennessee Plowboy." Ned claims that Craig's band had a poker game going on each and every day for fourteen years, and the piano player, John Gordy, was always the banker. Whenever they had to wait, and wherever they rode, one car or the back of the band bus was the poker room. There was a serious game of poker going on one night, and the Tennessee Plowboy was bent on kibitzing. Ned growled, "You're not going to kibitz on *this!* He told him to go back and ride with the WACs, and took hold of his elbow, put him off the bus, and shut the door after him—something Ned regrets having done to Eddy Arnold.

Francis Craig's ability to present a great number of first-class shows for the troops and, indeed, to hang a big band together for many years, came by the grace of his uncle's ownership of the National Life & Accident Company. Craig's father, just before he died, had made his brother promise to always take care of Francis.

The Hermitage Hotel was always teeming with soldiers, and the officers had their club on the mezzanine. Ned played down in the Green Room, which he called the "Green Hell Room," because it was so hot. They played every day for one and one-half hours at noon and for two hours at night, also filling three to five air spots each week over WSM, which was located two blocks away from the hotel.

One hot summer day, Bob Lamm was standing out on the curb taking a break. He was a tall redhead, about one hundred and ninety-five pounds, with clear blue eyes—the picture of health—except he was blind due to an accident at birth that damaged his optic nerve. Ned went out to join him, and noticed a warrant officer looking down from the balcony of the officers' club. He apparently believed Lamm was a "slacker," no doubt thinking *Here I go to war and he ain't doin' anything!* The officer descended the stairs, and Ned saw him standing by the revolving door of the hotel—looking at Bob with resentment. Guthrie didn't think anything would happen, but as they were talking the officer sneaked up behind them and sucker-punched Bob, hitting the side of his head. The army officer ran off yelling, "YOU 4-F SONOFABITCH!" Ned took out after him as fast as he could hollering, "YOU DIRTY BASTARD! YOU HIT A BLIND MAN! YOU KNOCKED HIM DOWN!" He gave up the chase and, fit to be tied, returned to check on Bob. He was still dazed and lying in the gutter. Bob's philosophical acceptance helped cool Ned down. Good thing, too. Their break was over.

Bob Lamm had been an immediate hit with everyone in Craig's band. Later in 1947, Jim Bullet (the announcer on the radio show) together with Francis Craig and his orchestra, made a souvenir recording of the theme song and released it on their own "Bullet" record label. On the flip side of "Red Rose," they used Craig's original tune "Near You." Craig had previously played it on the piano for Ned when it was an unnamed melody, and asked him what he thought of it. "It's catchy," Ned told him. He had said a mouthful. "Near You" shot Nashville into its first two million seller. It was followed by another hit called, "Beg Your Pardon." This was at a time when the Grand Old Opry was in its infancy, and two hits coming out of Nashville posed a threat to the New York record establishment. When they realized that they had been up-staged, RCA was the first company to send somebody into Nashville. RCA latched on to Eddy Arnold, and in no time Nashville became a major center for recording.

Francis Craig added to his fortune and, for a period of eleven months, he paid Bob Lamm two hundred dollars per week, and personally chauffeured Bob and his wife Florence from one first-class theatre to the next in his own limousine.

Ned received his "greetings" from the president in 1944. The closest he had gotten to military service was in the National Guard and broadcasting from army bases with Craig's band. His notice allowed thirty days before his date to report for induction, affording him little time to set his affairs in order. Guthrie moved his family back to Charleston. Gladys didn't drive, so he sold the car and bought a house. When the day arrived, he said his heartfelt good-byes to Ned Jr., Diane, and Gladys. Then he went off to war—or so he thought.

He had passed all the examinations at Camp Forest in Tullahoma, Tennessee, but at the induction center, while standing in line to get his bus ticket and assignment, the inductee directly in front of Ned made a petition. "My draft board is in Murphysboro, Tennessee," said the recruit, "and I request to leave for induction into the service with my home draft board."

The WAC replied, "You take this card, and go over there and sit on that bench, and a sergeant will be with you."

Ned had never heard of such a request, but when he heard "NEXT!" he stepped up and said, "My draft board is in

Charleston, West Virginia, and I request to leave for induction into the service with my home draft board." Sure enough, he was sent to the bench with the other guy. Ned was classified as 1-A, then sent back to Charleston to wait for his orders. He waited and waited, but by the time the Normandy Invasion had succeeded, Selective Service had issued an order not to send anybody over twenty-six years of age. Ned was thirty-four years old and, with a wife and two kids, he felt like his "Man" had been with him again.

While Guthrie had been waiting for "Uncle Sam," a union officer and a new club owner showed up at his door offering him an opportunity to put a band together for the Blue Room in Charleston. In August of 1944, this gig began—and lasted three years, three months, and thirteen days, working from eight o'clock to midnight all seven days of every week, and ending on New Year's Eve of 1947. During his "Blue Room Period," Ned had a bout with drinking and won. Counting all the gigs, before and after this one, over one hundred musicians would work under the name of the "Charlestonians." Ned hired the best players he could find and, at the Blue Room, ended up with a "monster" pianist named June Wolfe. His drummer, Steve Kaman (a Hungarian who knew polkas and emulated Gene Krupa), together with Ms. Wolfe, "kicked" trumpet players Fred Little and Dick Fultz. (They were, of course, the singers in the band!)

NED
PHOTOGRAPHER UNKNOWN

PART II

"They wanted to pay musicians what they wanted to pay them, and treat them the way they wanted to treat them. We were determined that was not going to be the way it was. And we went up against 'em."

—Kelly Castleberry

Panacea

Working in Nashville, Ned made friends at WSM with a bass player named George "Boozie" Cooper. He was a strong union man—president of the Nashville Local—and what Ned calls a *real* Southerner. Boozie could often be heard griping, "Those goddamn hillbilly musicians!" With considerable effort, he organized players in his jurisdiction. Ned had been in the union for twelve years, but hadn't attended many meetings. Boozie talked him into going to the Andrew Jackson Hotel, where Boozie's philosophy echoed in the halls at every meeting. His ideas boiled down to: "Don't associate with non-union musicians. Always try to get a contract. Don't let anybody give you a hard time. Take it to the Local, and the Local will try to do something about it."

Ned was deeply impressed with Boozie's sincerity, his zeal, and in particular, his effectiveness. He did well organizing musicians in Nashville, because he obtained agreements with radio stations to use union players. (This was prior to the Taft-

Hartley Act banning closed shop agreements.) When he had the majority of musicians under union jurisdiction, Boozie improved broadcast rates considerably, and organized the musicians at the Grand Old Opry. A piece of Boozie went home with Ned to Charleston, but he found his Local to be a far cry from an effective labor organization.

"We had an old man," recalls Guthrie, "our Secretary Rubin Blumberg. And honest to God, when he died he was one hundred and one years old. Well, when he retired, after he had been in fifty years—he didn't really retire—we gave him a gold watch, twice. He had moved to being ninety-three years of age, then! And eight years later is when he died—still (almost) the secretary—at one hundred and one years old. God bless his soul.

"Well," continued Ned, "the guy had his own ideas about running the union. He didn't believe in a picket line. He wanted to attend annual conventions of the American Federation of Musicians. And he didn't tell us—for twenty years of his going to conventions and us paying his way—that he received a per diem, as well as hotel expenses, from the Federation. Now he thought that was alright. 'Rube' learned to play the viola and baritone horn. He helped organize the Local in 1907, and played in the Burleu Theatre and other vaudeville houses. He was one of those kinds of musicians, but he had the union so screwed up that dance musicians had to oppose him. And believing in what Jimmy Petrillo had done (as an effective president to the Chicago Local), I said that we ought to have somebody like *that!* And we all would like the president to run the union, not the damn secretary!

"So, it took me a long time to fight that. And when anybody came in to join, he'd make friends with them and 'ace' them onto jobs—somebody who'd vote for him and oppose us. Well, it boiled down to the dance bands against the symphony, because he had the symphony orchestra wrapped around his fingers. Finally, I turned to the Federation in 1966, or 1967. I called and said, 'This man is losing his memory. If you don't come down here and do something about this, this Local is going to hell!' I was just Sergeant of Arms then, but I was a member of the Board of Directors. And finally, I got Bob Crothers—who was an assistant to President Davis—to send a fellow from New York named Harry Suber. This International Representative came in here for four or five days with us, and he finally understood that this man wasn't running it right—that he had begun to 'lose it.' So he convinced Rube to resign, and we had an election and elected a new secretary, Charley Hanna (the boy trumpeter who once caught Sousa's sneaky downbeat), and President Paul Nellen. The Local's Executive Board then rewrote the rule book to say that the executive officer would be the elected president—not the secretary—and this was ratified by the membership.

"Paul Nellen was a bassoon player," Guthrie went on, "a real good guy who played in the symphony. He was imported here by Union Carbide and worked in traffic control. He worked for management, but he had enough gumption and guts about the union to know that the symphony had been used to support Rubin Blumberg. They were doing the wrong thing, because the symphony players weren't getting any more money. At that time, they were working for five dollars per concert and four dollars for a rehearsal, and that was the entire symphony agreement. It wasn't even an agreement in 1967. There was no representation, no seniority—*nothing!* It just said in the wage book what the scale was. There was no contract in writing."

Union scale in a nightclub in Charleston was two dollars per night in the 1930's. It took Ned and other musicians five years to raise scale to four dollars, with leader pay doubled.

"So, we got scale up during Depression," said Guthrie, "but I can tell you it *never* would have gone up if we hadn't gotten the fellows to come to the union meetings, realize what was going on, and vote for a raise. There weren't that many musicians around Charleston like we have now, and not that many places to play. We couldn't make friends with everybody, but we weren't trying to run a popularity contest. We were trying to promote live music and organize musicians." Ned helped swell the membership of his Local, and convinced the Charleston Symphony members to strike the radio station. They established a unionized symphony, and everybody who played in it had to have a union card, including the conductor.

Challenging the Planning Commission on zoning laws was Ned's first confrontation that made the newspapers. Musicians in Charleston wanted to buy a grand old house on Kanawha Boulevard to use for their headquarters. It was an imposing building that was two and one-half stories high with nineteen rooms and a full basement. Built by one of the coal barons at the turn of the century, this old house was perfect for the Local. But, a banker lived in an adjacent house, and that appeared to have something to do with the attitude of the local politicians. They were intent on denying the union. Guthrie claims that what was said was, "We're not going to have any musicians and 'niggers' playing in this building 'n' teachin' lessons!" Guthrie extrapolates, "I'm not going to say who said it, but he did say it. He was on the Municipal Planning Commission."

So, Ned marched up to city hall and told the mayor about it, saying, "Okay! Your zoning board can have its way about it. We won't have our union office there, but there is no way to keep me from buying this building for a union home as a sixty thousand dollar investment. I've got the money. The man wants to sell. So we won't have any union meetings there. *But!*

70

Our union bylaws say that the sergeant of arms is the keeper of the door, and so we'll move him in there to keep our place! And he's black! And he's got *five* kids!"

The mayor gasped, "You wouldn't do that!"

"The hell I wouldn't!" snapped Ned. And having said that, he turned on his heel and left the mayor.

This happened on a Friday morning at about ten-thirty. Two-thirty Friday afternoon, Ned received a telephone call from the mayor's office. His secretary told Ned that he should put the request in on Monday morning to the Planning Commission and said, "You'll get the okay to have the building as the union office. We don't want to have a decree or issue here from the mayor's office. He wants you to go through proper channels, again. So you put it in Monday and you'll get it before the week's over."

Ned Guthrie—still obviously tickled with himself, his eyes in a kind of bulging delight—brags, *"That's twistin' the tail!"*

AMERICAN FEDERATION OF MUSICIANS
CHARLESTON LOCAL 136
INFORMATIONAL PICKET LINE

MEL GILLISPIE, SAXOPHONE; ED COOK, DRUMS; LOUIS ALBRIGHT,
AFL INTERNATIONAL FIELD REPRESENTATIVE; BILL RADER, TROMBONE;
JOHN VAN CAMP, TRUMPET; ROBIN NEAL, KEYBOARDS; KELLY CASTLEBERRY,
SAXOPHONE; PATTI GREGG, VIOLA; MRS. DAVID MCCLANAHAN, DAVID
MCCLANAHAN, DRUMS; LOUIS REINACHER, TRUMPET;
PRESIDENT NED GUTHRIE, SAXOPHONE; JIM BEANE, TRUMPET.
PHOTOGRAPHER UNKNOWN

On the Other Side
of the Counter

Mr. Withrow—sole proprietor of the Withrow Music Company in Charleston, where Ned Guthrie taught music lessons for fourteen years—often razzed Ned about his union involvements. Ned received the same treatment from his stepfather, Father Mack (the company man). He, more or less, "got a pass" from his stepson. Mack was family. "Old Man" Withrow, however, was another matter. He and Ned were constantly at odds over one thing or another. Here was a West Virginian musician and gung ho union man working side by side with a right-wing conservative member of the Charleston Chamber of Commerce—a former grocery store owner, a deacon in the Methodist Church—a salesman who had bought a music store. Ned rented studio space from him and, in Ned's candid view, "Withrow didn't know B-flat from bullshit!"

Although he utilized Ned's expertise with instruments,

Withrow bought a C-melody saxophone on his own from a sailor for twenty dollars in 1948. Believing it was a tenor sax, he thought he'd made a real score. When Ned came into the store, Withrow proudly showed his purchase, saying, "What d'ya think of that? Not bad, eh?"

Ned smiled and razzed, "What did you buy *that* for? They haven't used those since 1917!" The national election was the following day, and Ned knew he had Withrow "going," so he threw in, "Truman's going to *win!*"

On political matters, Withrow often retaliated by reading aloud the latest labor-bashing article by his favorite columnist, Westbrook Pegler—while Ned grimaced. But Ned's prediction sent him to the newspaper to quote the latest poll. Clearly, Dewey was ahead. *"Everybody* says so," retorted Republican Withrow.

"Well," advanced Ned, "maybe you'd like to make a little wager—say five dollars?"

Withrow wasn't a betting man, but "You're darn *right* I will!" just popped out of his mouth.

Ned taught in Boone County at a coal camp the next day. On the drive home he heard it on the radio: "TRUMAN WINS!" Triumphantly grinning from ear-to-ear, he showed up early the next morning to collect from Withrow. Still chuckling after forty-four years, Ned recalls, "That one almost killed 'im! It did put him in bed for five days."

Age caught up with Withrow in 1953. As prescribed by his will, the Withrow Music Company was liquidated—and Guthrie was left without a studio. There were about eight hundred dollars worth of drumsticks left over, along with some old sheet music, drumheads, and other miscellaneous items in this old—now abandoned—music store.

Guthrie knew he could get the trade (people would come back to that location) so he called up his trumpet player, Jim

Beane.

"Jim," Ned asked, "do you want to go halves with me in a music store?"

"We can't do that!" replied Jim.

"Sure we can!" assured Ned. "It'll take people a long, long time to find out I'm not really part of Guthrie, Morris & Campbell Company (owned by Ned's uncle). That's got a *good* credit rating."

Ned did get his uncle to give them good references and advise them, and could officially say he was their business consultant. "You can look him up in Dunn & Bradstreet," Ned would tell the doubters.

Ned had only six hundred and fifty-six dollars and Jim Beane borrowed five hundred dollars. That's how they started out in the business. When Ned was asked later on, "Would you do it all over again?" he hastily replied, "No! We didn't know what we were getting into." Jim Beane just gasped, *"Oh SHIT!"*

Guthrie and Beane rented a little hole-in-the-wall next door to the old music store for ninety dollars per month. Three college buddies—who had been in the Psi Delta Fraternity with Ned—provided their expertise, and a friend of Jim Beane's also helped. Two of them were musicians who understood what they faced in the way of competition. There were five music stores in Charleston when trombonist and fraternity brother Paul Carney, president of the Dunbar Lumber Company, saw what was going on and said, "Hell, we'll just build you a music store here. You can get anything you want on credit." Arthur Ostrin—a violinist and a football tackle, now owner of the Ostrin Electric Company—did the wiring in the studio. Lawrence Haggerty wrote up the insurance policy, and Jim's friend, a drummer named Gene Lowe—who worked as an artist and layout man for the state—designed the interior of the building. Together, they turned the "Guthrie & Beane Music Company" into what Ned remembers as "a real fine palace." Gladys would be the cashier and chief "cook 'n' bottle washer" while the men were out 'n' about selling instruments, teaching, or playing gigs. Without her help, it would have been a "no go," and soon after the doors opened they hired Lula Treem, their bookkeeper. She plodded through eight years of this business, and Lucille Pauley did books and taxes for the next fourteen years. (Jim says she kept the best books in West Virginia.) When Paul Nellen became president to the Charleston Local, and business was no longer conducted in Secretary Blumberg's office, the union membership voted to rent a room for twenty-five dollars per month adjacent to the Guthrie & Beane Music Company. Traffic created by musicians coming and going was a great asset to the store. All systems were "GO!"

Jim got along better with band instructors and customers than did Ned. "If there was *any* bullshit," says Jim Beane, "Ned would tell 'em right to their face. Nobody would fool with him. He'd hit you—or throw somethin' at you." Some internal adjustments were in order, and Ned became the inside man of the business. Jim was the outside man—each in his forte, or so it seemed at the time. It wasn't a strict system, and Ned turned out to be a good salesman. But as Beane put it, "He did it *unorthodox!*"

Many people who worked for Union Carbide frequented the music store, and most often they'd say, "I'm with the company," as though everyone should naturally assume it was Union Carbide. Both Ned and Jim knew what they meant— they wanted a *one-half off* discount on everything! It was irritating, especially to Ned. One morning, first thing, a Union Carbide guy came in, and Jim (who usually arrived around ten-thirty or so, after Ned) hadn't had his coffee yet. Then Ned showed up. As he walked through the door, Jim (somewhat capriciously) dumped "Mr. Carbide" into Ned's lap. Sure enough, the customer announced, "I'm with the company, and I'm lookin' for a good used piano."

Ned, who generally teased, "What company is that?" acquired an odd smile and said, "Come with me."

As they descended the basement steps into the bowels of the building, Beane could hear his business partner gruffly utter, "There is no such thing. There hasn't been for years. They've all been bought years ago. You want one for half price? There *ain't* no such thing! There hasn't been for years—only a few uprights." Pointing to an upright, Ned proudly exclaimed, "See! There's a *nice* one!"

"No," the guy says, "my wife wants a little one."

"There *aren't* any little ones!" growled Ned.

"I don't *want* a new one!" insisted the customer. "I want a *used* one!"

"*Whatsamatter?*" Ned snapped. "YOU GOT A USED KID?"

When Ned and his exasperated customer came up from the basement, "Mr. Carbide" quickly left.

Secretly amused, Jim asked, "What did you do to that man?"

Ned grumbled, "I asked him if he had a used kid. I'm tired of hearing that *Carbide* line!"

In retrospect, Beane maintains, "He was right, though. People say they want to give their kids a musical education, then get a cheap piano that won't even hold a tune!" Jim just shook his head as he added, "You shouldn't be *that* right in business, but that's the way it was."

Two years later, the two of them were driving around Charleston looking for a Christmas tree, and Ned spotted that same Carbide guy moonlighting, selling trees in a lot. Ned kept insisting that he wanted a cheaper tree. "Mr. Carbide" didn't recognize Ned until he started insisting on a "used" tree. Jim Beane maintains that there is much humor in what Ned does, and he has a memory like an elephant.

It was said that Guthrie and Beane built their business off the union. Ned admits that he exploited his card. West Virginia is a strong union state, and his card kept him out of jail a few times (when he was speeding to a gig and got caught). It also sold instruments. They would go up to a worker's house and say, "Here's my card—*oops!*—that's my union card. Here's my business card." The standard reaction was "Come on in."

Jim Beane felt he couldn't teach at first, but Ned got him into it, and Jim proved to be a fine teacher. All told, Ned taught private music lessons continuously for thirty-eight years. He taught mostly the single reed instruments, but also did well teaching flute, trumpet, trombone, and drums.

One of Ned's steady trumpet students came in one day and said, "Mr. Guthrie, I've got to change my lesson to Saturday morning. I can't come in on Fridays."

"Oh, why is that?" asked Ned.

He replied, "Well, I'm going to play basketball at Chelyan Junior High."

Ned didn't want to lose his pupil. His first reaction was to say, "I think you'd do better in the band. You'll never make a basketball player." (22,192 professional points later that was "Mr. Clutch"—also called Jerry West, whose name was honored in 1979 by the NBA Naismith Memorial Hall of Fame.)

Guthrie put the first sticks in Butch Miles's hands. That is, he sold him sticks and a snare drum for forty-five dollars, and threw in five drum lessons. When Ned heard how Miles took to drumming, he instructed his mother, "You're going to have to get this kid his drums," then gave her boy over to his able band drummer, Frank Thompson. Ned started Butch out, but Frank straightened him out.

Frank, incidentally, was African-American. When they brought him in to teach in the store, Ned and Jim had talked it over for a few days before taking him on, not knowing how it would affect their business. It didn't do a thing, and it was Frank Thompson who taught Butch Miles. Butch went on to play with Count Basie.

Everything was going along at a busy pace—even though nobody was getting rich—when Internal Revenue Service agents invaded the "joint" to audit the books. Ned and Jim weren't worried. Their books were as straight as a rail, or at least they should have been. They had hired both a book-keeper *and* a CPA when they first went into business. *No problem.*

The IRS went back three years. The audit dragged on and on, and after three weeks of solid auditing had transpired, Jim ventured to ask, "Who's gonna' pay our bookkeeper? She can't do anything else. All she's doing is handin' *you* stuff!" (No answer.) Jim pressed on, "Are we guilty until proven innocent?"

"Yeah," said the "federale" without looking up, "in tax cases you are."

Beane cussed him out. Guthrie was mad too, but their protests were ignored. Even while being chastised, "Mr. IRS" responded like a pro and continued auditing away.

When six weeks had passed, and the last ledger had been thumped shut, the IRS agent rose to his full stature and announced that the Guthrie & Beane Music Company owed the IRS *twenty dollars!*

"**WHAT!**" exploded Beane. But before he could utter another sound in protest, an agent turned to Ned to say, "Ned, you've been paying all these musicians without taking out withholding tax." (Suddenly, it was a "whole new ball game.")

According to Beane, "Ned had gone to the IRS in the *first*

place, and had said, 'I want to set up my band, since it's a partnership.' And, they advised him *not* to take out Social Security and withholding. So we had a partnership band. The IRS guy's boss had set Ned up, because he immediately hit Ned with a prepared bill for something like nine thousand dollars in back taxes, plus accumulated interest and penalties."

Guthrie obtained the help of a good tax lawyer who was a CPA and appealed it. It went up the ranks of the IRS. They finally sent down some new agents, and forty-two jobbing musicians got up early and came into the store to be questioned and sign affidavits. That's a considerable number of musicians, and Ned quickly took advantage of the resulting confusion—as IRS agents tried to say he was a contractor—by answering questions with questions.[6] Soon, nobody was making any sense. The IRS agents reportedly left with glazed eyes, and Jim's face lit up as he recalled that the last "federale" exiting the door said, "I never want to *see* this place again!" The feeling was mutual. Ned had to pay his lawyer even though the case was ruled in his favor, and the IRS didn't send them money for their bookkeeper. Jim grumbles, "Nobody said I'm sorry, or nothin'!"

Two decades later, the Guthrie & Beane Music Company closed its doors after twenty-two years of operation. It was a busy shop, though still not profitable enough to support two families. Ned says—over some of Jim's protestations—that he did the wise thing and sold their store at a profit to "Herbert's."

Dave Herbert and Dave Herbert, Jr. own Herbert's. Their business card is imprinted: "Herbert's, *where music is fun.*" When asked about the Guthrie & Beane Music Company, Dave Herbert, Jr. grinned and said, "They were competition, but my father started Herbert's in 1936. We outlasted 'em!"

Moon Pies and RC's

Worldorld War II scooped into service most every jazz musician in the country. Jazz players were hard to come by, and bebop charts laid down by artists like "Dizzy" and "Bird" required training and dexterity. Consequently, Jim Beane was thirteen years old when he answered a late evening knock on the door from several black musicians—Earl Tate, Bill Johnson, and some others—asking if he was the trumpet player in the Charleston High School Band. (For one thing, Jim could play loudly, and they knew he could read.) Jim said that he was the guy, so they then asked if they could speak with his mother. She wasn't home, but Jim's grandmother emerged from the kitchen to see what the heck was going on.

They wanted to take Jim and teach him jazz, and they had a Saturday night gig to offer. Jim figured that his grandmother would say no, but they also went into a "rap" about how Jim wouldn't be tempted to drink. Perhaps because she was a school teacher (realizing educational possibilities), she surprised the hell out of Jim by asking him if he wanted to do it. His "YES!" was as loud as his playing. The musicians took good care of him, as promised. When there was a bad fight, Jim's spot was behind the upright piano. He admits that he was sometimes scared, on many occasions the only white there. Jim loved the music, and learned jazz and blues because they took him in.

"Mixed bands" weren't exactly in style in West Virginia, yet there never was a black local musicians' union in Charleston. Unlike a good number of towns and cities throughout America, the Charleston Local was integrated as early as 1936.

That year, Ned's Charlestonians needed a piano player who could "fake" well. They didn't have enough money to buy a library, so Guthrie was scouting for somebody who could *play.* He found a piano player—a black musician who said that he would join the Union.

Ned talked to the owner of the Rathskeller who was a gambler and a nice boss. He told Ned, "I don't care if he's black. Can he play?" This owner, however, didn't want any socializing with white women. Having gotten past the owner, Ned took his sideman over to Secretary Blumberg's office. Rube, incidentally, owned many rental properties. He told them it would be up to President Crumb. George Crumb asked, "Did the secretary say it was alright?" Ned told him that it was alright with Bloomberg if it was alright with him. Crumb "chewed" on it for a minute. "Well," began the president, "you know West Virginia is more southern than it is northern. He'll have to pay the twenty-five dollars initiation fee all at once—up front. He can join and have a card, but he can't come to meetings."

"Well," replied Ned (not liking what he was hearing) "I don't think he cares about that. What he wants is a job to play." At the next union meeting, every member in attendance voted to take the piano player in as a union brother.

This piano player could "stand up and play backwards." It wasn't long before a white waitress started chasing him—and that was the end of that—until nineteen years later in 1955, when Ned hired percussionist Frank Thompson and a singer named Jo Baby. Frank played with the Charlestonians for twelve years, and Jo Baby sang with them for fifteen—singing everything from blues and jazz to tunes by Sam Cook and James Brown.

One week before a booking, a lady dean at the University of Richmond wired Ned requesting him to eliminate Jo Baby, saying that she didn't want a black female vocalist to be prominent on the stage. Some sorority girls, who had heard her at the German Club and the Cotillion Club, wanted to hear Jo Baby sing at their Ring Dance. They had plenty to say about it, and Ned wasn't sparing any words with the Dean—so the band played on.

The subject of Frank Thompson came up in a similar scenario for a gig in Kingsport, Tennessee, a one-nighter show and dance. Ned was told that all the musicians had to be white, because it was in Kingsport. Ned retorted, "This is 1959, not 1954. Frank goes, or we don't go!" That was the first such decision that had to be made by the booker. He took a chance, and let the band members worry about Frank. It was tricky and nervous, but Jim Hetzer (the booker) helped the Charlestonians break the color line in Kingsport.

One time a sponsor forgot to make eating arrangements for the band at a dinner gig. This was during the days when many restaurants, even on Summers Street in downtown Charleston, displayed "WHITE ONLY" signs. Guthrie and his guitarist, Fred Bredice, physically dragged Frank into the dining room of the Daniel Boone Hotel to eat with the rest of the band. He didn't want to go, but go he did. They broke the color line at

Daniel Boone's, although Guthrie says, "You don't know how many dirty looks and threats I got by using black musicians."[7]

"With Ned," comments Jim Beane, "we had a black singer, a black drummer, *and* a black bass player. We'd go down to Matewan or Williamson, or someplace further south—*couldn't eat!* We'd eat Moon Pies and RC's, because we wouldn't eat if they couldn't. Restaurant owners would be sorry, but they didn't want to lose their customers. In 1950, they thought we were crazy. But if you can play, we don't care what color you are."

Guthrie believes that good musicians don't pay attention to the skin or the name, and they can tell exactly what's in each others minds by how the music is played—the way you put things together. Friendships are made on that basis. He suggests that it would be wonderful if we could be like that in other ways.

As late as 1961, an agent's letter to Guthrie included the instructions: ". . . Also asked if the college provided dressing rooms for you and the band for the concert. Then you would have the time to drive downtown (Jefferson Hotel) and the colored folks go to Slaughter's Hotel where they can get rooms and meals."

Below the Smith & Wesson Line

U p river eighty miles from Charleston, a coal miner's daughter was shot by a bullet fired from a mountainside. There was a strike going on in Widen in 1955, and the Charlestonians were booked there for a school prom. Ned knew there was going to be more trouble, and was worried.

There was only one way to get there by car. Over the last twenty miles they would be vulnerable on a mountain ridge road where you could look down and see lightning during a storm. The other way was by company train, but somebody had blown it up! It didn't look good, and Ned was scared to go—but he didn't want to give up a gig. So the band took a vote, and everybody voted to go except the singer Lora Barnett, whose family didn't want her to go.

Ned telephoned the principal of the school. He told Ned that the band would be provided with an armed escort. They were to meet at a place called Dundon, located on the Elk River at the beginning of that ridge road. He promised that the band would be able to get by the pickets, except Guthrie demanded that one car of strikers be there to say they were welcome. The principal objected saying they weren't striking kids, but Ned wasn't taking his word on anything, not this time.

Two cars of musicians were met at Dundon by three cars, and a convoy was formed. Headed by a company car, the sheriff's car was second in line, followed by the band cars. The rear sentry car was chock-full of coal miners.

Armed escort or not, they were stopped and examined. It was "uptight," and the guitarist actually vomited. Nonetheless, they descended safely to the coal camp school, and a good gig was played.

Every Wednesday Ned drove forty miles to teach and hold a band rehearsal in Prenter, West Virginia. One week, none of the students showed up for their lessons. Ned wasn't surprised. A strike had started up, and miners don't buy much or do anything extra during a strike. Guthrie says that they might buy a barrel of flour, bake bread, and make pancakes. That may be all they have to eat, but they stay with the strike until they win. As in the song "I Owe My Soul To The Company Store," Ned reports, "I was generally paid in two dollar bills, because everything costs twice as much in a coal camp store." He had a talk with the principal to let her know that he would wait until after the strike to be paid for the lessons.

For fourteen weeks the strike continued, and every one of his students showed up for their lessons. After the first paychecks came in, Ned had more two dollar bills than he could stuff in his pockets. He always had respect for the miners' honesty. Still, coal camp gigs (most gigs, for that matter) could get "hairy."

At one coal town, Guthrie's trumpet man was "eyeballed"

by a miner's girlfriend. Her guy was "drunk as a skunk." So "naturally," he slugged Ned (while he was playing the Beer Barrel Polka) right in the face—hard, breaking his glasses. Then he took off like a bat out of hell. Ned tried to find him but couldn't, so he went back and finished the gig. He later received a telegram from the manager of the hall promising to "keep the troublemakers out."

"There's a lot of violence over in Kentucky, too," explained Ned. "They are always suspicious of strangers. In Corbin, I started to put my sax case up on a table next to the bandstand. It was my first night with Del Willis and his Kentucky Wildcats. The tenor player said, 'You can't put your case there. That's the gun table.' I thought he was crazy, but soon people came in, and men *and* their dates started piling their pistols on that table, in full view of everybody. That meant that you were unarmed ladies and gentlemen."

"Yeah," adds Jim Beane, "when you'd come, you'd put your gun on the table. Then if you had a fight, you wouldn't *kill* anybody. If you got in a fight and shot somebody—they'd *hang* your ass. It was okay to fight, just don't *shoot* anybody!" snorted Jim. "Knock his teeth out, but don't kill 'im."

"Southern West Virginia? I don't know," continued Jim. "They had shootin's down there most every week. That's the stompin' grounds of the Hatfields and the McCoys—still around! Jitterbuggin' at a club called "The Tunnel Inn" in Williamson, one Hatfield would throw his gal up in the air so that her heels would make marks on the ceiling. The ceiling looked almost like it was designed that way. They have a good ol' time."

At a gig in Kentucky, Ned was on a break, standing in a garage among several hundred tires piled up high. There was a little opening where the musicians and some other people were tipping a jug of moonshine. It was crowded, and a bare lightbulb was hanging directly over Ned's dome, making it difficult for Ned to get the jug up high enough to take a swig. Some guy whipped out his pistol quick as lightning and— **POW!**—blasted out that light bulb. Several people then pulled guns and started shooting at whatever. Ned hit the dirt floor in his tuxedo, and he and Jack Evans managed to elevate a pile of tires enough to scoot under them—and crawled out of there in time to return to the bandstand to play, while guns were still popping. Jim Beane remarked, "That would get your attention, wouldn't it? Every musician has a hundred tales like that to tell—but is it funny?" Jim ponders. "We're lucky enough not to get killed!"

CHARLESTONIANS
Jo Baby, Frank Thompson, Ned Guthrie
Photograph by Tech Studio

Johnny Come Latelies

During the 1950's and 1960's, the music scene in Charleston underwent changes with the "Private Liquor Club Bill." As soon as the West Virginia State Legislature passed it, more nightclubs opened. Ned saw the need for a major drive to organize, and President Paul Nellen gave him free rein to form "The Downtown Committee." For the next four years, this committee had two members—Ned Guthrie and his protégé, Kelly Castleberry (now deceased). Kelly gave up music as a full-time occupation to help Ned as a business agent for the Local. Guthrie says, "I stole him away from his daddy's real estate business."

They devised a system with business agents calling on the clubs to establish union presence. Kelly was the principle agent. One other representative, plus a few female members, helped him, and all the agents carried credentials when they popped in at the clubs. Some operators tried to keep them out on the basis that they owned "private" clubs. Guthrie took that issue to the Liquor Control Commission, and it ruled that nothing could prevent union officials from conferring with musicians. That's all they needed. It was honorable to check cards and contracts, and see that everything was okay. The first thing Ned drilled into the agents was never to take money from musicians at gigs—not for *any* reason. He felt this would send the right message to both owners and musicians.

"We started organizing our territory," recalled Kelly, "organizing right down the center, then started expanding. A lot of undesirable people, who had been involved in all types of businesses, had just gotten into the club business. We had to deal with a lot of those people. Some of them organized, and we had several instances of threats—and of actually being shot at.

"Before Ned became president of the Local in 1973, he still had his orchestra. He came home from working that orchestra one night, and he had a regular routine of coming home, relaxing a little bit, then going to sleep. And he turned out the light. I think he decided he wanted a bowl of ice cream, so he turned around and went back into the kitchen. And they shot the windows out! And that was a close call. Ned is tough and was undaunted by these things until they began to touch home. It was very upsetting for Ned when Gladys received obscene phone calls because of his union activity—his *home* fired upon with gun blasts!

"These club owners," Kelly went on, "didn't want to deal with the union. They didn't want anybody interfering in their way of doing business. They wanted to pay musicians what they wanted to pay them, and treat 'em the way they wanted to treat them. We were determined that was *not* the way it *was*. And we went up against 'em."

Threatening telephone calls awakened Ned and Gladys almost every night. The calls would start at midnight and continue into the early morning hours. Somebody mistook

Ned's neighbor's Volvo for his car and vandalized it. The Guthrie residence was fired upon on three occasions. Ned contacted the Federation for help, and assistance came in the way of advice. Kelly benefited from several discussions he had with a high official who was in contact with all of the locals.

They were not the only members having problems with club owners. As Kelly remembered it, this official pushed his nose and ear over to look like a pug and said, "When all I got was a bellow, I'd hang up." He spoke of a widespread problem that started in Kansas City in the early 1930's. As long as musicians played the job and took care of business, club owners would sign contracts if they liked the performances. Performers, however, couldn't quit the job and work somewhere else. Musicians were often, in effect, held hostage—particularly if the owners *liked* what they were doing.

This official had received many telephone threats, and told Kelly that he reluctantly carried a "piece" for awhile. He'd tell them, "Make the first one a good one, because now it's a two way street!" then hang up. He was also approached in his office on three occasions with bribes. To inform his superior about it, he had established a signal with his secretary so she could bear witness.

He asked Kelly if they had contacted the police department to put protection on Ned's house, and wanted to know if they had any friends in government who might have influence with the operators. He advised that they were not always as bad as they would like you to think, but agreed that they were violent. His initial recommendation was to "stay away." Don't go around the owners or do anything to anger them. They were told to "play it cool," which wasn't very good advice—because that didn't stop them.

The best counsel they received was to get in touch with the liquor controllers and any friends they might have in the labor movement, people who do business with nightclubs. Liquor licenses might be withheld or revoked if clubs were having labor disputes.

Ned and Kelly first went to see their State Attorney. "They knew who we were dealing with," said Kelly. "One time I was in a nightclub that was between where my office was and home. At that time, I was working for the State Labor Federation as well as being secretary-treasurer of the Charleston Local. On my way home I stopped to have a drink first, or whatever. The prosecuting attorney called me there at the bar and said, 'I think you should go straight home, and I'll send somebody down to talk to you.' Then he asked, 'Aren't you concerned how I knew where you were?' I said, 'It did cross my mind.'

"One of his investigators came out. They had received word—through their internal ways of getting information through their sources—that Ned and I were going to be killed in a short period of time. It wasn't either one of us. I think that they just wanted to let the union know that they didn't want to deal with us the way we wanted to deal with them.

"Ned referred to them as 'Johnny Come Latelies' in the club business," continued Kelly. "For years we went without any liquor-by-the-drink law. We had bootleggers that ran after-hours joints—basically the same people that had been in Charleston for years. We never had any problems with them. They paid the bands. They signed the contracts. They were alright. But these people that came in and tried to take over the business with the passage of the law were dangerous."

Aided by an attorney, the Charleston Local blocked several licenses from being issued to undesirables. Stories like these are common among musicians who serve as union officials. Many Locals were once named "The Musicians Mutual Protective Association."

Where's Uncle Willie?

Sleepy Jeffers was a well-loved man who warmed the hearts of West Virginians, young and old alike. An old-time comedian, he'd put a cap on his head, blacken his teeth, and become "Uncle Willie." He performed with his wife Honey and a guy named Roscoe Schwartz, a singer of serious songs to balance out Sleepy's act. (Diane Virginia Guthrie played the Lowrey organ in a six-piece country band that accompanied Uncle Willie when he appeared on Buddy Starcher's TV show.)

Sleepy's character, "Uncle Willie," was on the verge of national fame. All over West Virginia—if someone could get Uncle Willie to open their store or car wash—people would flock to see him like bees to honey. That was his livelihood.

In February of 1974, Sleepy Jeffers contacted Ned at the Union Hall to tell him that an out-of-state conglomerate had bought out the TV and radio station, and had announced a new policy to discontinue live entertainment. Sleepy told Ned, "I would like to keep my group. Now I went out and sold my

TV show to a sponsor for six hundred and fifty dollars. That's for a once a week, one hour show. The station wants five hundred and fifty dollars of that. That only leaves one hundred dollars—and that's under union scale. What can I do? I don't work nightclubs. Ned, if we go off the air, we're dead."

Ned thought for a moment and said, "Well, we'll just set a new scale to fit that. We want to keep you on the air."

Sleepy took a new contract to the station manager, who refused to sign it. Sleepy needed and wanted a contract. He needed good musicians, and wanted professional respect. In Ned's view, he deserved both. Besides, Sleepy Jeffers had worked there under union contracts for the last twelve years.

Ned telephoned the station and the manager told him, "I'm not signing any contract, Mr. Guthrie, and I'm not going to have any union agent coming in my studio—not at *any* time."

Guthrie told him, "We have never sent anybody over there to check out any band at your TV or radio station. If I want to check out Willie's act, I'd just sit at home in my living room, watch it on TV, and see who's on the air."

"Well, I'm not signing any contract!" shot back the broadcaster. "And if you try to get me to sign it, I'll *fire* Sleepy, and it will be you *and* your union's fault that he loses his job! Furthermore, I'll replace him with reruns of the Beverly Hillbillies! And that will cost me only twenty-five dollars per show!"

Ned asked, "You know about the Lea Act, don't you?"

"Yes," replied the broadcaster, "I know about it."

The die was cast. With that having been said, their conversation ended. If Ned Guthrie had said, "Yes, but—," he would have been subject to a fine and imprisonment in a federal penitentiary. The Lea Act was U.S. Labor Law. He was helpless.

As for Uncle Willie, he was doomed to obscurity. He went

off the air when the station manager fired Sleepy Jeffers—and terminated another family show, the "Jackie Oblinger Show." They simply took the musicians' recorded products and stuck them in the programming, displacing the talented live shows.

Ned wasn't sure what he could do about a federal statute, but he had won a close election against a good man to become president of the Charleston Local. In addition to Kanawha County, his jurisdiction reached into Logan, Mingo, Boone, Raleigh, Fayette, Nicholas, Clay, and Putnam Counties. Feeling the weight of his new responsibilities, and unaccustomed to backing off, Ned Guthrie made a silent vow to do *something* about that law.

CARTOON BY FRED L. PACKER
COURTESY OF NEW YORK DAILY NEWS

PART III

You take my life when you do take
the means whereby I live.

—Shakespeare

The Party is Over
Story of the Lea Act

Ned Guthrie was eleven years old when radio broadcasting came into being. He remembers how radio stations started popping up all over the country. They featured live music and, in the musical Roaring Twenties, an hour or two of broadcasting was news.

"Musicians didn't grow up on radio," reminds Guthrie. "Radio grew up on musicians. Station managers came to musicians to ask them to broadcast because the old 78 RPM records of the day were too scratchy and noisy."

Music makers worked for "exposure" for two years before they demanded and acquired broadcasting fees in 1922. The networks soon developed radio shows with fifteen-, sixteen-, and twenty-piece orchestras, and big bands flourished on the public airways. "There will never be anything that would take the place of radio," says Guthrie, "because we had about fifteen years of the greatest successes in show business, and all benefited from it who were capable of playing on it. It was a way of life."

Musicians experienced severe unemployment problems resulting from the Great Depression, and Prohibition compounded their job losses. By the time it was repealed, radios and jukeboxes had taken the place of untold numbers of musicians in service businesses.

The first crushing defeat that musicians suffered, however, occurred because of automation in the theatre. In 1925, one-fifth of the membership of the American Federation of Musicians played for shows and silent films. Threatened with job displacement by the "talkies," the Federation under President Weber launched a national campaign to protect twenty-two thousand prestigious theatre positions (based on an appeal to the "aesthetic sense" of the movie-going public). It failed miserably. Within eight years of the first showing of *The Jazz Singer,* theatre managers had jettisoned 17,900 accomplished musicians. They spilled out of the theatres into the bars—and some made it onto the airways—but many of them left the profession to teach or "sell shoes."

The "talkies" phenomenon created an illusion of inevitability concerning the use of technology in the music business. Concern for the rate of automation never existed in the broadcast industry, and each new technological advancement in sound recordings cut off more and more musicians from the airways.

Martin Block's *Make Believe Ballroom* (first aired in 1935 on WNEW in New York City) proved that the public would listen to records on radio.[8] More importantly for the time, *it spurred record sales,* and a panic spread among musicians who demanded, "If you want to use our music for profit-making, then use *musicians,* not our recordings!"

Musicians felt themselves to be the same as authors who write stories. Another person doesn't have the right to take

100

their stories and print them—and in the process, displace the writers—preventing them from ever publishing again. Lacking copyright protection for their recorded renditions and interpretations, musicians labeled their records, "FOR HOME USE ONLY."

Broadcasters had organized themselves into the National Association of Broadcasters by 1922, and throughout the 1930's they collectively ignored the musicians' labels. In 1939, musicians stopped recording. The issue went to an appellate court, and in 1940 it ruled that *artists' rights ended with the sale of their records*. The entire canned music business could then sell and resell their recordings *forever*.

Since musicians were the *sine qua non* of the record business, the record companies decided to make a deal. The Federation was to receive a one and one-fourth cent royalty on the sale of a record, and eight and one-half cents for an album. This was placed in a trust fund. Musicians couldn't stop the commercial use of their creations in jukeboxes, or on the airways, so record manufacturers were to provide what Guthrie terms "crumbs"—that paid some unemployed musicians to perform free to the public in schools, hospitals, and parks.

Since the jukebox continued to take over the musicians' workplace (as it had taken over the Rathskeller), the Federation consequently initiated a second recording ban in 1942. The annual convention (as union supreme rule) upheld this ban as it had the previous one, and recording sessions ground to a halt in the United States, Cuba, Puerto Rico, and Argentina. Union musicians in England also stopped making records for export to America.[9]

Trouble in the broadcast industry continued. If the Federation felt that the number of hired musicians was not in line with a radio station's profits, the station would have to hire either more musicians or, in many instances, nonperforming standbys (featherbedding). This practice was legal, at that time, though the idea of someone getting paid *not* to work was controversial. (Ned Guthrie reasons, "I cannot adjust to the Government paying farmers not to grow tobacco or cotton in agriculture, yet say standby musicians was wrong.") The Federation had leverage with small stations dependent on a network for programming—by threatening to strike the network involved in the commercial enterprise of "networking." In 1941, the Federation forbade its members to play cooperatively broadcasted hookups. The previous year it had pressured broadcasters to stop broadcasting "sponsored" programs of military bands, and also curtailed foreign and student broadcasts.

The Federation has traditionally stood against the use of children and teenage musicians when there is commercial value to the broadcast. It wants music students to be able to broadcast, but not in competition with *current professional* musicians. It draws a line between "educational" and "entertainment" broadcasts, the latter being the domain of the professional musician. As it is, citizen musicians pay taxes for schools and the military, ironically subsidizing their competition.

These recording bans and other actions by the Federation received unusually bad press. Though it's been said that the mainstream of morale during World War II was the music, when the Federation mandated playing the National Anthem before, and after, all public events, *that* was characterized as "a rendering unto Caesar" by writers making sport of the union president's middle name. This union rule caused trouble in the bars, and was rescinded within six months after it was initiated. (Guthrie remembers a local character who would hang out all night at the Rathskeller, an aged Jewish tailor from Russia. He'd have a few drinks, and begin dancing by himself, like a graceful Russian dancer—even when the "Star Spangled Banner" was played. Ned discouraged him at first, but the owner didn't mind. That changed when more than one out of town serviceman became offended and started a fight. Ned says they were *bad* fights, and the boss ordered him to stop playing the national anthem. Ned stopped when the order was rescinded.)

One of the main tenets of American society—that the government should not compete with private industry—was forgotten as Americans perceived *any* interference with the military as "unpatriotic." Foreign and student broadcasts (though apparently not broadcasts by professionals) were considered "cultural." With kids involved, obstruction of student broadcasts became a "mom 'n' apple pie" issue—with musicians vulnerably stranded "on the wrong side of Mother."

All hell broke loose when Government agencies were unleashed against musicians. The Federation was investigated by Congress, and the F.B.I., sniffing for nonexistent crimes, weaseled its way into the fracas. The Justice Department attacked the ban with an injunction procedure, but in accordance with the Wagner and Norris LaGuardia Acts, this was struck down in a District Court in a decision upheld by the U.S. Supreme Court. Since this was an industry versus labor dispute, the recording ban was not technically a strike. Contracts had expired. There was no agreement, and the dispute was a private sector matter.

The next thing to happen was that the president of the Federation was "called on the carpet" before a subcommittee of the Senate Committee on Interstate Commerce. President James C. Petrillo testified that he sought negotiations. The trust fund (used to benefit musicians that the industry did not employ) was no longer acceptable to record companies. Petrillo told the House Labor Committee that the trust fund was not needed if the recordings were "FOR HOME USE ONLY." At one point, Petrillo informed Congress, "The party is over. We quit!"[10]

A rebuffed "Uncle Sam" was not prepared to keep his nose out of *this* private sector dispute. The "musician problem" was unsuccessfully turned over to the U.S. Conciliation Service, bounced to the National War Board in 1943, and at some point, scrutinized by the War Production Board—even though this ban didn't affect music recorded for the war effort. *Every* government agency involved exceeded its jurisdiction by ordering musicians back to work. (Petrillo would later challenge the government saying something to the effect, "Okay Congressman! You just make a law to make us go to work. Chew on *that* one for a while!")

The Executive Branch was heard from next. President Franklin Delano Roosevelt (who often had taken flak from his enemies for maintaining a "studied silence" during industry vs. labor disputes) sent one telegram to the Federation requesting an end to the ban. By that time, all but two of the big recording companies had settled. Feeling that "what's good for the goose is good for the gander," and to be fair to approximately one hundred companies that had already settled, the Federation stayed with the ban. It simply didn't make sense to record oneself out of work.

Petrillo was also called before the Congressional House's Un-American Activities Committee. One panel member, Representative Richard Nixon, told Jimmy Petrillo, "I won't be happy until I see you behind bars."[11] (Petrillo was appropriately found to be innocent of any Un-American activities. In 1972, when the Watergate scandal unmasked Nixon's unveracity, Petrillo sent him a telegram that read, "Dear Dick, It looks like you're going to make it first," signed "Jim.")

On the "other side of the fence" this recording ban was not

the only problem record manufacturers faced in the 1940's. In its 1941 contract negotiations, the American Society of Composers, Authors, and Publishers (ASCAP) wanted a "bigger piece of the pie." Sensing a dilemma on the horizon, broadcasters formed Broadcast Music Incorporated (BMI), and in 1941, they boycotted ASCAP music. Most established composers were members of ASCAP, so while retaining ten percent of the collected royalties, BMI corralled country and western bands, and journeyed into the area of ethnic music as well as rhythm 'n' blues, precursor of the 1950's record boom, rock 'n' roll. Also prevalent during the ASCAP Boycott by the broadcasters were BMI versions of public domain music—such as Stephen Foster and the ever royalty-free "classics."[12]

Record companies scrambled to stockpile records prior to the ban, and raided their archives to release old stock. They tried recording singers a cappella (some singers singing sounds to imitate instruments). The Federation threw a monkey wrench into that action by reminding vocalists that, after the ban ended, their actions would be taken into account. With little success, record companies also tried recording instruments that the Union had not yet admitted to legitimacy—such as ocarinas, harmonicas, spoons, bucket-bass, whistlers, and one-man bands.

In the midst of these difficulties, however, the record companies were helped by a shortage of shellac caused by the war. Imported from India, shellac was a key ingredient in the composition of records before vinyl copolymer came into use. Its shortage appears to have kept executives of the phonograph industry from seriously pursuing a settlement to the ban.[13] *Downbeat* magazine reported that one executive claimed the ban was the best thing that happened to the waxing business—in view of the shellac shortage. "We don't have to record a hundred tunes now with a batch of bands just to be sure we have next month's best seller in our catalogue."[14]

The National Association of Broadcasters enlisted the services of a "hired gun" attorney named Sydney Kaye. He devised an insidious scheme that met with a unanimous vote of confidence from the NAB's member stations.[15] Kaye's plan was basically a simple one: Since the only deterrent to automation of the public airways was the American Federation of Musicians, *destroy it by assassinating the character of its president.* Only one broadcaster withheld his vote in protest against this conspiracy. Samuel R. Rosenbaum addressed the 3rd District Meeting of the NAB on October 19th of 1942. He said, in part:

> Let the jukebox do as we did and do its own share to remedy the conditions against which, in my opinion, the *musicians have a just complaint.*
>
> The handling of the Petrillo situation by the National Association of Broadcasters is a masterpiece of ineptitude.
>
> ... Our Association should never have taken the leadership in a fight against the musicians. Their fight is not against us primarily, but principally against the jukebox barons and the record manufacturers. *We have engaged counsel to master-mind the campaign and we have hired a high-pressure publicity firm which is inspiring the national flood of news stories, editorials and cartoons against Petrillo.*
>
> While I admire the strategy, it is our paws that are getting scorched. If we keep it up we will be badly burned.... Having entered into it, we are allowing our name to be seriously damaged by letting it be used in a form of *labor baiting* and *labor leader smearing*—which is a relic of a past generation. It may end up losing us all the gains we have achieved an industry in 20 years of fair dealing with labor. ...
>
> *With the entire press of the United States at our disposal, and with powerful branches of Government lending themselves to the effort,* all we have been able to think of is to *attack the integrity and personal character of one labor leader* who happens to be a vigorous and outspoken agent of his craft. ... The only remedy we have proposed is the old reactionary slogan, *"Keep Everything As Is."* ... the court

action which was started with insufficient forethought and inadequate preparation may put a clamp on us which will discredit everybody who had any part in this cynical proceeding. . . . It is at least to the credit of the Department that the action was limited to a civil proceeding instead of firing off a terrifying blank cartridge with a criminal indictment.

Petrillo's objectives also require legislation and it is probably just as true that any legislation he wants would stir up the *underlying problem of patents, copyrights, and restraint of trade. . . .*

I appear to be the only broadcaster who has seen this thing differently from the start.[16] [Author's emphasis.]

Downbeat recognized that most vehement criticisms of Petrillo were written by "labor baiters," but acknowledged that many of the union's problems stemmed from Petrillo's blunt conduct with the press and the dictatorial powers granted him in the Federation's constitution.[17] Petrillo's power was no greater than that of most labor leaders or, according to one legislator, "the head of a well-run corporation."[18] *Downbeat* embraced musicians' rights to endorse a royalty on records to benefit the union's membership and a tax on jukeboxes—but this trade journal's opinion was lost in a torrent of assaults on musicians. They appeared in newspapers, magazines, special bulletins, pamphlets, and by teenage Anti-Petrillo clubs that started up around the country.

With World War II as a backdrop, among the broadcasters' "Programs for Victory" emerged the idea of a "Second Front," a program consisting of daytime radio announcements regarding the "second front" being *right here at home.* The news media characterized Petrillo as an autocratic and illiterate leader—a bully. He was ridiculed as the "Tsar," the "chieftain," the "half-pint dictator," and often characterized as "a cannon cracker looking for a match." *Life* magazine headlined an article with, "PETRILLO, Little Caesar of Symphony and Swing Wages War on Juke Boxes, Musician Children and

107

Military Bands." *Life* went on to say, ". . . sitting at his desk, he suggests an elderly frog that has eaten a big and somewhat bitter dragonfly. . . ."[19] *Current Biography* stated that Petrillo " . . . murders the Kings English" and says, "He has been called the 'Mussolini of music . . . a pettifogging parasite'. . . ."[20] Lacking violence or criminality of any kind to pin on musicians or their president, widely read columnist Westbrook Pegler (Guthrie says, "He made me so damn mad!") cleverly mixed up stories about the criminal activity of some Teamsters with the legal (now controversial) labor practices of the musicians—moving from one to the other as though they were one. Cleverly concocted, this guilt by association was reinforced by *Collier's* use of photos of Petrillo and some striking musicians—placed beside and under Pegler's damning headline, "THIEVES WITH UNION CARDS."[21] (Pegler tried to protect himself and *Collier's* by grudgingly ending his article saying, "Petrillo is, to my almost certain knowledge and to my strong convictions, not a crook.") A broadcaster in St. Paul, Minnesota damned Petrillo and the musicians further by writing:

> During a time when the entire civilized world is engaged in a battle against the worst form of tyranny ever known—Hitlerism—the radio industry, which is giving its time, ingenuity, and men to America's tremendous war effort, is beset by a form of tyranny which is in its own selfish domineering the public-be-damned way as cruel and brutal as Hitlerism itself.
>
> I speak of Petrilloism. James Caesar Petrillo has become the Fuhrer of 140,000 musicians in this country. He has grown powerful and rich by the exercise of an iron hand by which he now attempts to wreck an entire industry.[22]

A gush of humiliating cartoons lambasted and demonized Petrillo, and his name became interchangeable with the word "gangster." (Ned Guthrie painfully remembers being called gangster. During that time in Charleston, more than once when entering a nightclub, he heard someone hiss, *"Petrillo!"*)

The broadcasters' hired gun was on target with his plan. According to a poll taken in 1942, three-fourths of the American people disapproved of Petrillo's actions, and over seventy percent of them wanted his American Federation of Musicians' head chopped off by Congress. The "trout in the milk" was that many newspapers were interpreting Petrillo's power and actions as the natural outcome of the New Deal's Supreme Court and the New Deal's political agents in Congress.[23]

The 1942 recording ban dragged on for two years, ending at the same time shellac became available again in abundance. Musicians' gains, in retrospect, were minimal. They clung to their trust fund—the "crumbs" of two hard-won battles.

The canned music wars, however, were not over. Senator Vandenberg induced the Federal Communications Commission (FCC) to demand a statement from Petrillo explaining the Federation's interference with student broadcasts at a music camp in Interlochen, Michigan.

Labor was "in for it" and musicians had been set up to take the first "hit." Having been the minority party in Congress for fourteen years, Republicans stormed into control of both Houses of Congress in 1946 with an intent to dismantle Franklin Roosevelt's New Deal labor laws. It wasn't long before a bill came through the House of Representatives—a duplicate to a bill introduced by Senator Vandenberg that had already passed the Senate.

"They are the demands of a criminal class," snarled (ex-district attorney) Representative Clarence Frederick Lea. "A self-respecting nation cannot afford to treat them otherwise."[24] He was talking on the Floor of the House of Representatives about musicians, and his bill was an "anti-racketeering act" subtitled, "the Anti-Petrillo Law" (distinguishing Petrillo's name to be the first, perhaps the only, labor leader's name—in the entire mosaic of labor law—to be used on a federal statute). It was to "prohibit certain practices affecting radio broadcasting," but its vague wording and terms like "evil practices" signaled some legislators that Lea's Bill was intended to outlaw the strike.

Lea's camp fell under pressure from a handful of opponents and a "shell game" ensued. Involving complete shifts of position, infantile semantics, and word games by proponents, they hammered at the theme set by the broadcasters' vilifications aimed at "Caesar." It led an exasperated Senator Taylor to cry out, "I have tried to find out what the language in the bill means. Nobody seems to know. It contains the words 'other means.' Nobody knows what those words mean, and no one has been able to tell me whether the threat of a strike is coercion."[25]

Legislators in the House of Representatives had the same problem. Representative Vito Marcantonio pointed out that, "The American people have been subjected to an expenditure of $1,500,000 on the part of the National Association of Broadcasters to popularize Mr. Petrillo's middle name."[26]

Representative Rabin tried to clear the air by offering an amendment. It read, "Nothing herein contained shall prohibit the right to strike for any objective which may be lawfully obtained through negotiations." His proposal was voted down as a "crippling amendment."[27]

Mr. Marcantonio was an avid opponent to Lea's camp. In his remarks on the Floor of the House he said:

> Let us see what is involved here. When the average musician makes a record, he is really helping to put himself out of business. He is paid $20 or $30 for the making of that record. That record is used by the broadcasting companies, not for the cultural edification of anyone, but it is used to make money, more money, and more profit. It is played on

programs advertising this or that item. The broadcasting companies are being paid for those programs. What does the American musician get for the playing of that record? Under this bill, what do you do? You say to the American musician that if he asks for a quarter of a cent royalty, and if he says, 'Unless you give me a quarter of a cent royalty on that record, I am going to refuse to work,' under the language of this bill that means he is violating the law. Further, his refusal to work under those conditions constitutes a criminal offense under this bill. If there ever was a racket, this bill is a racket. If there ever was anything immoral, this bill is immoral. This bill takes money out of the pocket of the American musician and puts it in the pockets of the broadcasters. You cannot get away from that. You can stand here and talk about burying Petrillo all you want, but as a matter of fact, you are burying the American musician. . . ."[28]

Representative Brown answered Marcantonio with:

. . . This Bill, of course, affects James Caesar Petrillo.
. . . You are told this legislation will reduce the compensation of musicians. It does nothing of the kind; for it does not reduce the compensation of any musician who actually plays music. Those of us who have studied this measure know that better than two-thirds of the members of Mr. Petrillo's musicians' organization are not working musicians.[29]

In the following year, the House Labor Committee found that seven percent of union musicians were employed, and stated that this *might* be an indication it is difficult to find employment.

The legislators put "teeth" into the Lea Act. Any employee's refusal to work in order to acquire more workers on the job site was designated as the crime of "coercion." What the criminal penalties boiled down to was this: any expressed objection to the whim of a broadcaster made by a musician could land him or her in a federal penitentiary for one year on a misdemeanor charge with a one thousand dollar fine. Two or more musicians involved, a drummer and singer for instance, or more likely, a musician and a union official (as was the case with Sleepy Jeffers and Ned Guthrie) was "conspiracy." That charge carried a five-year prison term, a fine of five thousand dollars, and, of course, the stigma of a felon—if only but triggered by a broadcaster's complaint.

Time ran out on deliberations. The Lea Act passed the House of Representatives with a ten-to-one vote, and the legislators cheered and stomped their feet. Nevertheless, this Anti-Petrillo Law's fate was now in the hands of a piano player. Once a member of the musicians' union, President Harry Truman—apparently without reservation—signed Lea's bill on the 16th of April in 1946, and the Lea Act became United States Law.

When it came to bad press, Petrillo was known to have thrown up his hands and ask, "What can I do?" With this law, the integrity of the American Federation of Musicians was on the line—not to mention the airways' work. The Federation's Executive Board tested the constitutionality of the Lea Act by demanding that Radio Station WAAF in Chicago add three additional musicians to its staff orchestra. The constitutional issues then went to court—and Petrillo went to jail. Henry Kaiser, the Federation's Chief Counsel, got him out of there the following morning after Petrillo, not without humor, flamboyantly whipped out his wallet and peeled off ten crisp one hundred dollar bills to the court for bail.[30]

The case went into the U.S. District Court in Chicago, and the Honorable Judge Walter LeBuy (after denying the American Civil Liberties Union a brief) ruled that the Lea Act transgressed the Constitution on three accounts: it violated the musicians' rights of free speech, equal protection under the law, and freedom from slavery and involuntary servitude.

Musicians believed that they had won *something* from Government, but the Justice Department appealed under a special rule that sent constitutional issues directly to the U.S. Supreme Court. Feeling confident, musicians applauded this action by the Justice Department. The musicians' attorney, Henry Kaiser, filed a brief in 1947 for *U.S. v. Petrillo*. It read, in part:

> . . . The statute does not lay down anything like a consistent or comprehensive national policy on labor relations in the radio broadcasting industry. It is, rather, an expression of unrestrained vindictiveness, as witness the vituperative attacks with which the Report and debates abound. . . . Congressional discussion even sank to the low level of making derisive sport of appellee's name.
>
> This unreasoned, bitter assault upon a labor organization of some 200,000 citizens can be explained only as the expression of an enraged prejudice that has been carefully nurtured and spread by the owners of the broadcasting industry whose inordinate profits were threatened with some reduction by the normal demands and activities of those whose training, skill and energy substantially contributed to the success of that industry.
>
> Their owners, banded together in a powerful national association, with virtually unlimited funds and with direct control over the access to the nation's radios and newspapers, the major avenues of public communications, were firmly resolved to smash the Musicians' Union for the simple reason that it, like any other union worthy of its name, was vigorously attempting to preserve and extend the economic welfare of its members.
>
> The method they adopted was an elaborate propaganda campaign of abuse and vilification designed to inflame the people and the Congress of the United States and thereby enlist the sovereign power of our national government in support of their efforts to perpetuate their dominant economic position. The law approved on April 16, 1946 eloquently attests to the complete success of their well-laid plans and energetic efforts.
>
> Far from doing a "disservice" to other labor unions, far from acting "outrageously" or arbitrarily, the American Federation of Musicians has been in the forefront of a *social and economic contest whose outcome is vital to trade union-*

ism. The "weapons" it has employed have always and ever been completely peaceful ones of refusal to work, non-violent picketing, and verbal appeals to its fellow unionists and to its other friends.

A fundamental reason for the formation of labor organizations is the need and the desire on the part of workers, helpless as individuals, to obtain employment and to protect employment already obtained. Without employed membership the Musicians' Union, or any other union, would, of course, cease to exist. Collective bargaining, which is the declared policy of our Government, necessarily presupposes employment.

The American Federation of Musicians is, because of the circumstances in the industries in which its members work, particularly sensitive to abiding threats of unemployment. More than any other craftsmen in our economy are they subject to loss of jobs by less expensive labor.

The statute would stultify the obvious realities that have shaped the underlying policies of the Federal Government for many years. The underlying policy of the labor and social legislation of the last fifteen years was to create employment opportunities and to adopt other means that would minimize unemployment.

. . . there is no validity whatever in the assertions on the part of the supporters of the Lea Bill that defendant or any group of employees in the radio broadcasting industry had been engaged in evil practices. All they have done is to engage in controversies that are as old and familiar as the employer/employee relationship itself. These controversies are all aspects of the basic issue that exists the world over—the desire and effort on the part of owners and employers to obtain and maintain the widest possible margin of profit and the conflicting desire of employees to obtain and maintain the widest possible margin of security and gainful employment.

The contest in the radio broadcasting industry is particularly acute because the musician employees are peculiarly subject to displacement by the machines they make, because the industry is new (with little experience in the statesmanship of collective bargaining) and has made gigantic strides and profits in remarkably short time, and because added to the economic power of the industry is its strategic power to publicize and propagandize its own views and interests, a power greatly enhanced by the circumstances that *many broadcasting stations are owned and controlled by newspapers.* Making full and effective use of its extraordinary powers, the radio broadcasting industry has succeeded in unfairly weighting the issue in its own favor by receiving the aid of our Government in the form of the Lea Act. We assert that the aid thus given is repugnant to the Constitution of the United States.

The statute outlaws the simple strike, the peaceful picket, and all other "means" to achieve objectives which the statute itself expressly legitimates.

... The flagrantly one-sided approach of the statute is, we submit, explicable only in terms of the deliberate intention on the part of its sponsors to enlarge the prerogatives of the licensees and thereby enhance their profits.

The Supreme Court justices listened politely, then sent a jolting chill down the "spine of Labor," ruling the Lea Act to be constitutionally sound—however conceding that *"application of the Act could have such an effect."*[31]

"It was a lot of double-talk that the Supreme Court came out with, as I remember," says Hank Armantrout, a retired union official. "I think it is a classic example of the majority of 'em in the Supreme Court climbing up on a fence 'n' gettin' a-straddle of it."

"But here's the catch," advises Guthrie. "The Court said something to the effect that it was a bad law, however, Congress has the right to pass a bad law, just as when it passed Prohibition. We were playing for our own funeral, and if we complained and lifted the coffin lid up and said, 'Hey, you can't bury me like this!' they could jail you. They truly had that threat."

Before the fact, the harshest criticism of the Government came from within. In a Minority Report disfavoring Lea's Bill, Vito Marcantonio's concluding sentence reads:

If we permit ourselves to be stampeded by the outcry

against one individual into overriding the basic rights of the working people of this Nation, we will have betrayed the trust and confidence which has been placed in us by the American people.[32]

The 1947 Convention of the American Federation of Labor (AFL) voted to come to the musicians' aid, but the Taft-Hartley Act of 1947 destroyed maximum cooperation between unions. It outlawed sympathetic strikes and secondary boycotts. The trust fund was also outlawed, and the Taft-Hartley Act's closed shop provisions crippled the Federation's capacity to build a work force. Truman did veto the bill, but was overridden.[33]

If Robert Taft of the Taft Broadcasting Company didn't hold a "conflict of interest," one might assume that for all practical purposes there is no such thing in Congress. He had like company in Lyndon B. Johnson, Senator John Buckley, Representative Hugh Ike Shott, and Joe L. Smith—of KTBC, the Starr Broadcasting Company, WHIS, and WJLS, respectively. The latter two, incidentally, were from Ned Guthrie's home state.[34]

Outraged, musicians again dared to withhold services to record companies. Again, record companies stockpiled recordings prior to the ban. Many musicians broke this ban and, lacking the solidarity they once enjoyed, their ban soon unraveled. It ended when Attorney General Tom Clark ruled that the trust fund (now named the "Music Performance Trust Fund") was legal. The MPTF was saved when put in the hands of a third party—*a broadcaster*—none other than Samuel Rosenbaum (the one who had "spilled the beans" at that 3rd District meeting of the National Association of Broadcasters).

Broadcasters had had U.S. Government pave the way for excluding live music from radio station programming. They had won a great victory, and upwards of twenty thousand broadcasting positions on radio consequently faded into history. At the same time, the Lea Act illegalized any financial payment by broadcasters to musicians for the use of their recorded creations, perpetrating what Jay Victor of *Nation's Labor* terms, a "legalized embezzlement" (of the performers' would-be royalty payment).[35]

So returning to West Virginia—to Charleston, the Union Hall, and a determined but troubled Ned Guthrie: He had made a vow to do something about the Lea Act, and had been mulling over his and "Uncle Willy's" problem with it for many hours. Everyone had left, and it was getting dark as he locked up the hall and drove home to Gladys—still deep in thought.

Ned Guthrie and Hank Armantrout
Photography by Gail S. Rebhan

Decathlon

Ned could have been a great general, but around the house he's a big pussycat," says his daughter Diane. "I had him wrapped around my little finger, but then, so did mother. When I was a little girl he always had time for me—even when he was working all day and night at the store and playing gigs."

As the good father running Guthrie & Beane—as the salesman, the teacher, the bandleader, the performer, *and* the exceptionally active union official combined—even a workaholic like Ned Guthrie knew when something had to give. In 1973, he surrendered his Charlestonians to Mel Gillespie (head of the band department of West Virginia State College) saying, "I don't need a partnership. You take the band. The union business and the band are too much for me. I'll play when you need me." One year later the Guthrie & Beane Music Company was sold, and Ned confined his playing to occasional shows, circuses, and engagements with the Charleston Symphony Orchestra. He turned his attention to union matters, fully committing himself to getting the Lea Act repealed.

On this account, Ned was up against the powers that be. Paramount were an adverse Supreme Court ruling (on the books since 1947) and the Act itself—buried in the massive, mussy Communications Act. He would have to lobby an ignorant or indifferent—if not hostile—set of legislators, and the broadcast lobby and the "money people" would oppose him. Ned, however, felt this to be his calling—that his "Man" was with him.

An optimist at heart, Ned also felt that he had picked up a little political savvy along the way. A situation in the 1960's introduced him to the lobby game when several large taping facilities in West Virginia had begun the wholesale pirating of tapes. It developed like a fad. One such facility was located somewhere outside the city of Huntington. Another one was hidden in Kanawha County somewhere near Charleston. When an anti-piracy bill was introduced in the State senate, both Ned and Kelly Castleberry took keen interest to see it move through the State legislature and receive Governor Arch Moore's signature.

Moore also later helped Ned with a Theft of Services Bill, which made it illegal to stop payments on checks for service industry people. Introduced by State Senator Todd Kaufman (now a circuit court judge in Charleston), the bill was written up with musicians in mind, and Ned was the brain trust on it.

Guthrie had people tramping all over certain areas out in the woods to find the pirating plant. The Country Music Association in Nashville found out about the search and pitched in, but couldn't find it.

Crinkling his nose in disgust, Guthrie recapped how they could not prod the legislature to move on the piracy bill because one legislator from Cabell County had complained,

"Well, if this bill passes, then we can't copy tapes—and it will cause seventeen of my voters to lose their jobs."

"Man, that really hacked me!" exclaimed Guthrie. "I made remarks. That legislator was saying it's all right to steal from musicians! 'If we don't let them steal tapes, the stealers will be out of a job.' That's *horrible!*"

Ned was finally able to do something about the situation when the pirates started copying and selling a recording of a good, country singer-songwriter named Eddy Bailes, who played regularly in the lounge of the Heart of Town Restaurant and at Smiley's Motel in St. Albans. (Ned's granddaughter Robin was one of the backup singers and played keyboards in his combo.) When Ned learned that Governor Moore had had Eddy sing "This Is My West Virginia" at the annual West Virginia Day party in Washington, D.C. for the West Virginia Society, he knew that they could obtain Moore's help if they could find a pirated tape of Eddy's song. Mainly through the efforts of Business Agent Ed Cook, they found one copy and took it to Moore's office. Arch Moore immediately got on the Senate Judiciary Committee where the bill had been stuck. Shortly thereafter, that very legislator from Cabell County (less worried about his seventeen voters) rose on the senate floor in glorious indignation to announce, "We're going to pass this anti-piracy bill, BECAUSE THEY WILL *NOT* STEAL FROM EDDY BAILES!"

It took *only* five years to pass this bill, but Ned saw the value of legislation.

Ned also learned something about politics in 1970 when his daddy was on his deathbed. After World War II, Purple Hearts had been issued to wounded veterans of World War I, but for some reason Robert had never received his medal. Ned wrote a letter to the Commandant at Camp LeJeune, explaining who his father was and how he had been gassed at

Argonne. He ended it with, "He never got his Purple Heart and I want to know, by God, why not?" Robert's medal arrived within one week. It was his to have for a matter of days before he passed away. (Marines buried him with full military honors, and Jim Beane played graveside taps. Incidently, Robert's influence on Ned's half-brothers produced Air Force Airman First Class Earl McNider Guthrie and two Air Force Lieutenant Colonels. Fleetwood LeJeune Guthrie dropped paratroopers from the second plane in the first wave of the Normandy Invasion, and Harold Edward Guthrie became a fighter-bomber pilot, flying one hundred and two combat missions in Korea and Vietnam.

Ned had "stuck to *his* guns" in becoming a musician instead of a military man, and, having demanded his father's medal— and gotten it—he surmised that giving the truth to "the top" would back a man of power into a corner. He learned to take on the top brass, figuring that they are as good as they are— but if they were wrong, *he'd* be in the driver's seat.

So, in 1973, Ned launched his campaign to repeal the Lea Act. He had "REPEAL THE LEA ACT" T-shirts printed, wrote letters, made daily telephone calls, and started taking trips to Washington. A lone advocate for some time, he kept at it with the tenacity of a sixty-three year old man already known to be adamant about union matters and musicians' problems— whatever they might be. Jim Beane says of Ned, "He gets something into his craw, like this helping musicians. Even with guys he didn't get along with, he'd beat their family to the hospital to see if they needed anything. You might think he hated you, but he'd be the first to see you. He'd just want you to be straight and not pull any bullshit."

When a TV evangelist intoned, "Gospel musicians don't need a union, *our dues* are paid in Heaven!" Guthrie was undaunted. Spotting the troop bus idling in a loading zone with the door wide open, he bounded up into it and started doing some preaching of his own. His sermon was a long one (considering the circumstances) but funny—or at least taken so.

"Those are UNION musicians *up there!*" he declared. "There's no *scabs* in Heaven. What'd you think? Angels are *scabs?* The musicians on your TV show shall *ALL* have union cards! DO YOU UNDERSTAND?"

They got a kick out of Guthrie's sneak attack, and actually joined the Charleston Local. When the preacher found out about the Music Performance Trust Fund, he became known for "braggin' on the union."

Another time, a club owner from Montgomery in Fayette County threw a musician from Charleston out through the front plate glass window—and then had him jailed until he promised to pay for the broken window. The musician refused, and was spending his second day in jail when Ned found out about his plight, grabbed an attorney, drove thirty miles to Montgomery, sprung the musician, went to the club—and entered through the still unfixed broken window. Two henchmen were at the bar, and one of them conspicuously placed his revolver on the bar in a gesture meant to let him know they were armed. "We have guns, too," warned Guthrie (a bluff sufficient to provide thought for the two "heavies"). He turned to the owner—a formidable man who obviously wasn't taking much crap off of anyone—and said, "You signed a contract with this musician. You have a problem, you call me and we'll straighten it out. But don't you *ever* raise a hand in anger again to another musician in *this* union!" Ned is tough. He was in his sixties when he did that, and he was no less vehement when he flew to Washington to "kill the Lea dragon."

"The first three years I went to Washington," Ned admits, "I didn't want to see a congressman. I wanted to see President

Jimmy Carter! That's how dumb I was. Most people are like that. They'll go down to the police department and say, 'Bring up this case. Bring it up right now!' But that doesn't go in Washington. You don't do that to Congress. They tell you if, when, and what to do."

He seemed to be spinning his wheels, but one day an old acquaintance walked into his office who had frequented the Rathskeller to listen, and who played saxophone in the Charleston High School Band—years after Ned. His name was John Slack, and he had become a United States Congressman. He wanted Ned to explain what all this "Lea stuff" was about. Ned could hardly believe his good fortune. He whipped out a copy of the Lea Act. One might say it was passed from one "reed man" to the next, as Slack sat down to check it out. His eyes focused on it for some time as Ned rattled on about Uncle Willie's fall from the airways. John Slack suddenly stood up and exclaimed, "That's *wrong*, by George! We're going to do something about that. You come and see me in Washington."

That was it for Ned. He was on a roll now. As president of the Charleston Local he was a delegate to conventions. Fifteen states comprise the Southern Conference of locals, and it met two days before the main convention of the American Federation of Musicians. Guthrie obtained the support of the 1974 Southern Conference to offer the main convention a resolution to repeal the Lea Act.

Then things went haywire when an assistant to the Federation president became alarmed and left the conference—to scurry over to President Davis and squeal something to the effect that there was some hillbilly from West Virginia screwing everything up!

With that in mind, President Davis came to address the Southern Conference. He didn't start off with "Hello everybody."

"GENTLEMEN!" barked Davis. "I understand that from the ranks of the Southern Conference there is a movement to repeal the Lea Act." He paused and looked up at the ceiling, raised his fist high in the air, then smashed it down hard on the podium. *"The Lea Act is a fact of life and you're just going to have to live with it! It"s a waste of time!"* Davis (perhaps thinking he had dealt with the "Rebs") moved on to other issues, then retired from the conference.

From that moment on, Ned was "seeing red." He had been stabbed in the back by his own union, and could hardly contain himself. If there was a restrictive line of jurisdiction over national legislation not to be crossed by regional leadership, Ned crossed it in grand style when his turn to speak finally arrived. He challenged the delegates by saying, "That might be alright for a guy in New York City, who we elect to do that, but that's *not* the way it's going to be in West Virginia! We have a motto: *'Montani Semper Liberi!'* That means, 'Mountaineers Are *Always* Free!' And by God, I don't know what you people are going to do, but when I get back to West Virginia, I'm going to get *rid* of the Lea Act. I'm a free man!"

Marty Emerson (a superb trombonist, who was secretary-treasurer of the Federation, and would one day become its president) made a characteristically supportive, fraternal gesture by moving down from his designated chair on the dais to sit next to Ned on the floor. While Secretary Emerson was there, Ned asked for and was empowered with a voice in the *International Musician* (the monthly trade journal mailed to every member in America and Canada).

Ted Rube "Thumbs" Dreyer, a jazz pianist and assistant to three Federation presidents (a grizzled veteran of thirty conventions, now retired) states, "I just can't believe what happened, that Davis of all people wouldn't have espoused it. To speculate," continued Dreyer, "he was very much attached to Kaiser, our general counsel. He was very smart, wise, articulate, and just a great labor lawyer. Maybe that's what was going on at the time—something contrary to the efforts that were being exerted—that Ned wanted to introduce some cocky resolution contrary to what was going on. But hell, I don't know."

Guthrie returned to West Virginia more determined than ever, and reported in to John Slack. Slack taught him that a citizen does not have an automatic right to get a bill heard. "This country is run by committees," tutored Slack. "Laws are made by committees. You have to go to a committee and tell them the problem, and see that a majority of them believe it enough to schedule a hearing. Then you present your case with witnesses and evidence."

Ned was working on a shoestring, but kept plugging away lobbying the communications committees under the self-assumed title of "Chairman" of the "National Committee to Repeal the Lea Act." He kept his nose to the grindstone with a pushy exuberance that sometimes irritated those around him. Jim Beane, for one, referring to Ned's gung ho involvements, said, "I got so tired of hearing 'Lea Act,' I wouldn't listen to anything about it. We were in business together when it started. I'd be out selling instruments, maybe with a handful of contracts, and say 'I'm selling instruments out there!' He'd be on the phone so damn long I couldn't even talk to him! He'd call 'em, those politicians, and cuss 'em out. He'd say, 'Who do you think you're talking to? You *used* to play a horn? Well I play one *now* for Christ's sake! I just want a chance to go out and make a living like everybody else! You *think* about that, SIR!'"

Finally, Ned's exuberance failed him. He came into the Union Hall, went into his office, slumped in his desk chair and did nothing.

"I was so blue," he remembers. "I didn't have *any* money. And every time I used the office girl, I had to reimburse the Charleston Local for it."

Later at a convention, the president of a Western Local asked Ned, "If you had fifty thousand dollars could you get the Lea Act repealed?"

Ned answered, "You're damn right!"

This official raised only sixty dollars. Ninety-one-year-old Jimmy Petrillo mailed Ned his personal check for fifty dollars, and wished him luck. When Ned became chairman of the International Musicians Committee (via an appointment from Marty Emerson), the president of the Sacramento Local graciously handed over his per diem check for sixty-eight dollars to him at a committee luncheon. Other small checks trickled in, but the trickling trickled out. Such were Ned's groaning thoughts when the mail arrived with a five *thousand* dollar check from Secretary Lou Russo of the New York Local. Ned sighed and took a deep breath, then went to work.

From the start of his repeal drive, Ned maintained an ironclad rule to talk to at least one new person each day. In Washington he lobbied dozens of offices daily. All too often Ned would hear, "He won't be able to see you *for some time.*" Those words, "for some time," meant anything from twenty minutes to twenty hours. Sometimes it simply meant *GET LOST!* Guthrie's stock reply was, "That's fine. I've got the time. I'll wait." He'd hang in there for days if necessary, and when he spotted some senator or aide he had targeted entering an elevator, he'd cram himself in there with his face a matter of inches from theirs. Advantaged by a captive audience, he'd follow them to their car. Once in the office of a legislator, he'd scan the walls for a copy of the Bill of Rights, creating linkage between it and his equity issue by saying, "If that doesn't apply to musicians you're going to have to take that thing down off your wall, because they're not compatible!" (The implication was that he, Ned Guthrie, might stand up at any second and do that for them.) Convinced of the discriminatory aspects of the Lea Act, he wasn't the least bit apologetic about its repeal. *Demanding* is closer to it! He wouldn't be sloughed-off. More than a few legislators signed on to his bill to get him out of their offices, if not out of their lives. He'd show up early *every* day, or telephone incessantly. In an office new to him, he'd loudly announce, "Hi! I'm Ned Guthrie. I'M A MUSICIAN! Ya know, the *musicians'* union." Everyone would usually stop typing and look up to see Ned, all smiles, with his seersucker jacket, bizarre tie, and rumpled hat. He figured if somebody didn't resume typing—hanging back from the rest—there was a good chance they either played an instrument or knew someone who did. Anything to get going with it. He could be entertaining, a Southern charmer, and would sometimes "hang up" the office help with lighthearted stories and jokes (tidbits on repeal ever worming their way into his dissertations).

Sometimes he encountered *the enemy* (a legislator who flatly stood against musicians' civil rights). At more than one of these meetings, according to Mark Massagli, Ned "clicked the wheels" of government by consuming certain foods and loitering flatulently by the receptionist's desk.

Ned the lobbyist was generally liked by staffers and their bosses, but as Jim Beane would put it, "He did it unorthodox." Ned could be downright obnoxious or insulting, and purposefully angered some legislators and other people to obtain their undivided attention. Nevertheless, he was usually diplomatic. Ned just worked straight from the shoulder with the saving grace of humor, and knew his issue so well that he could look a "legal eagle" in the eye without blinking. "Hell," says George Daugherty (a case lawyer with a downtown office in Charleston), "I didn't explain the law to Ned. He educated *me* as to the law. Not just the Lea and Taft-Hartley Acts, but the history as well. He got me to join the union when I was a saw player. I wore a T-Shirt, and accompanied Ned on a couple of trips. No, that was a one-man deal."

Daugherty knew what Ned was up against. He was an entertainer as well as an attorney—a guitar and musical saw player and singer-songwriter known as "The Earl of Elkview." One time, when he had been flirting with a career in acting, he had come up against the power structure himself.

A major network with a keen interest in historical documentaries had decided to broadcast a drama about the Buffalo Creek Flood in a three-or four-night series. One hundred and eighteen people had been killed due to the alleged negligence of a major coal company. The story focused on the lawyer named Larry Stern, from the firm of Arnold & Porter in the District of Columbia, who represented all of the survivors. Frank Perry was hired as the director, and Anthony Perkins was to play the part of Attorney Stern. Rights were purchased, a cast was hired, and a considerable amount of money was spent.

Daugherty got his chance when someone suggested that it might be inappropriate for Perry to play the part of a down-home West Virginia judge. At a dramatic point in the story—after the coal company has been threatening to drag the trial out for several years—Judge Hall instructed the lawyers, in no uncertain terms, that *all* briefs will be in by such 'n' such a time, and, looking the coal company attorney in the eye, set a trial date, saying, *"That* is *that!"* As an attorney, a West Virginian, and an actor, Daugherty was awarded the part—but one week before the network was expected in West Virginia the show was called off. George received a telephone call from a secretary who said, "We have tickets purchased, but the whole thing has been canceled because of the threat of retaliation against the network by business interests. They have the power."

On another front, Guthrie decided to have a talk with Senator Robert C. Byrd of West Virginia about his appearances as a fiddler with non-union musicians at state rallies and other events. Ned asked Jan Campbell (the bandleader he had worked for in the 1930's) to go on a trip with him so the two of them could talk to the senator. (Byrd, by the way, is an accomplished country fiddler who has appeared on Grand Old Opry and Hee Haw.) Ned explained to the senator how his actions embarrassed the Union, and ended up making him an honorary member of the Charleston Local. Byrd later attended union meetings, and when speaking to musicians he often jokes, "Ned Guthrie got me into the musicians' union, and I've been sorry ever since." It wasn't long before Guthrie garnered Byrd's backing on the repeal of the Lea Act. Musicians had gained a valuable friend in Washington.

At the 1978 Convention of the American Federation of Musicians, the repeal movement got a boost. In a speech about "performance rights" and "performers' rights" the president of the Western Conference, Henry "Hank" Armantrout, called for a resolution to stop recording until musicians obtained copyright protection for their recordings and *some* musicians were employed by radio stations. Ned sat with Mark Massagli. Turning to him, Ned remarked, "Look at him out there. He's beating his head against the stone wall. Even if we would strike and not make any records, it's against the law now to go and try to talk about employment at the stations if the station manager says, 'Not interested!'"

Massagli nodded his head in agreement.

"What we have to do," Guthrie continued, "is get rid of the Lea Act before we can do *anything!*"

Massagli told Ned, "You better get in touch with him. Give him a call. He's got influence on the West Coast."

When Ned returned to Charleston, one of the first things he did was write a letter to Hank Armantrout.

Hank had "been around the block." His musical career began in the 1920's when he was a fledgling banjo player, later switching to upright bass. He hit the road with his older brothers' band as a union card-carrying kid. He kept his musical career and traveled the United States, eventually marrying and settling down in Ohio. Armantrout finally moved to the greater Los Angeles area, and became an active union official holding numerous titles and positions throughout the years. When he understood what was happening, he became co-chairman to the National Committee to Repeal the Lea Act, which linked the Southern and Western Conferences. His influence drew in the Western Locals, and Hank proved to be a good fund raiser. Now retired, he says, "Really, Ned did all the legwork. I helped him some with a couple of trips over there to Washington—one at my own expense. There were wide expanses of distance between us, but we both visited each other's conferences once a year. Anyway, I did raise money. The Federation didn't give us money. As a matter of fact, the Federation has been going 'in the red' for several years now.

"Ned's tough, a magnificent man in diplomatic language," continued Armantrout, "and he's a convincing salesman, too. I never had direct contact with the lawmakers of the country—but you never saw such a bunch of fence-ridin'. Y'know, they listen to ya, and you think you have them convinced— then they say, 'It sounds like something ought to be done. I'll give it every consideration.' The difference is if they *sign* the bill! I must say, Ned Guthrie has got patience."

Ned and Hank split up the United States into two playing

fields with the Mississippi River forming the division. Ned's committee was becoming "national" in the true sense of the word as locals all over America began falling in line with Ned's grass roots scheme for the repeal.

In 1976, when Hal Davis died unexpectedly of a heart attack, Victor Fuentealba became the president of the Federation. Armantrout said of him, "He didn't have much use for me *or* Ned." Like Davis, he didn't see fit to fund the repeal drive. "Not one damn dollar!" as both Ned and Hank expressed it.

Their committee didn't have Political Action Committee (PAC) money to feed the legislative "kitty." They believed that if they could explain to legislators the true story of what happened to musicians (considering that it had been thirty years since anybody had broached the subject), the lawmakers would see the unconstitutionality of the Lea Act. They believed in "the system" and the Constitution, and that once legislators knew the truth, they would give musicians their rights. "They will," Ned often warned, "or else they'll have to take the Bill of Rights down off their walls." They also banked on the simple, significant fact that not every legislator owns a radio station.

A stroke of luck came on a return trip from Washington in 1978 when by chance Ned sat next to (necessarily meaning he conversed at length with) a successful twenty-six-year-old native West Virginian industrialist, Roy Labon Pittman.

Roy Pittman, co-owner of the Windsor-Pittman Coal Company, Inc. and the Windsor-Pittman Chemical Company, Inc., was an exceptional young man, by anyone's standards. He was an excellent businessman whose cultural and humanitarian outlook included saving Charleston University's Music Department. He formed the Charleston Conservatory of Music and Fine Arts, and served as its president. Using his influence, he established the "Natural Resources Foundation of West Virginia," a trust fund that derived revenue from operators of heavy industry. He then established therapy for physically handicapped children at the Conservatory. (The University took the Conservatory under its wing in 1987.) Pittman also concerned himself with an abandoned stash of hospital equipment that was discovered wrapped in Cosmoline in a cave in West Virginia. (It was one of a number of precautions taken by the Government during World War II, and the last of its kind.) With it he established a two hundred and fifty bed hospital in the Philippines. Pittman was founder of the Myasthenia Gravis Foundation of Southern West Virginia, was also a board member of the Morris Memorial United Methodist Church, and donated money to the Mayo Clinic. He also ran twice on the Republican ticket—bidding for the job of secretary of state, and once for a seat in the state senate.

After meeting Ned Guthrie, Roy Pittman returned home and told his parents, "I met a most unusual man on the plane. He told me about the Lea Act. That's the most awful thing I've ever heard." His father, Heber Pittman (a self-made man in the chemical industry), agreed with him, and financed many of the trips Roy would make with Ned to Washington to "knock down doors." Roy was getting a kick out of learning to be a politician and a lobbyist. In one fervent day, he and Ned lobbied all of one hundred congressional offices.

Ned started picking up some highly influential people through Roy—such as Director Norman Fagen, of the West Virginia Division of Culture and History, and Governor John D. Rockefeller IV. They took the pertinent messages about the Lea Act to state government in West Virginia. Roy also knew Abe Fortas, a former Associate Justice of the U.S. Supreme Court (whose hobby was playing violoncello). Abe told Roy that this law, if challenged, would be defeated in Congress because it was unconstitutional. Ned, of course, knew that Lea's law was a "scum-bum affair," but it was encouraging to hear it from the "horse's mouth." Among other things, Roy Pittman went to see Ralph Nader, who was taking an interest in the public airways. Roy told Ned that Nader appeared sympathetic, though nothing ever came of it. On his own, Roy drove his sports car all the way to Portland, Maine to observe the 1980 Convention of the Federation. He secured a great deal of free publicity there for the repeal.

Roy would later uncover a serious problem that would haunt Ned's efforts in Washington. In an attempt to obtain the testimony of a star performer before a congressional committee, Roy wrote letters and made dozens of calls to a vocalist of world-renown. (Legislators have a high regard for testimony by "star" performers. They often request such testimony before acting on legislation affecting *all* musicians—sometimes as a stall tactic.) The performer wanted to do it, but his manager interfered to protect his "star's" career from an industry backlash. This "gag" control over a performer's free speech posed an ongoing "Catch-22" situation for Ned.

When Congressman John Slack first went to Washington, he gained an audience with Sam Rayburn. According to Slack's friend, George Daugherty, Slack had told Rayburn, "I'm just a kid from West Virginia—just got elected. I want to get on here and be effective."

Rayburn told him, "John, just be quiet. Some people come up here and make a big splash about it. If you really want to be effective in Congress, just get in there and work and keep quiet. Stay out of the controversy."

Slack took Rayburn's advice, and soon chaired the powerful Appropriations and Military Committees—gaining considerable trust and earning respect from his peers. Tip O'Neil would later say of him that his word was his bond. Slack avoided controversy, but he was far from mute on the subject of the Lea Act. He introduced a repeal bill in the House of Representatives, and it was referred to the Commerce Committee. Senator Randolph followed suit, and his bill was referred to the Senate Commerce Committee—establishing a beachhead for Guthrie and the musicians in both Houses of Congress.

A bill "in committee" generally remains filed until somebody or something starts making noise about it. This time around, most every local in the country was committed to the repeal drive. The Federation's affiliation with the American Federation of Labor and the Congress of Industrial Organizations (AFL-CIO) garnered help from their Department of Professional Employees (DPE). Guthrie's twig was growing into a tree as musicians were drawn into what many of them—six years previously—had ridiculed as "Guthrie's Folly." With locals beating the drum for repeal, even a broadcaster popped into the repeal effort (by not opposing it). She was Senator Nancy Kassebaum, daughter of Alf Landon (the Governor of Kansas who ran against F.D.R. and lost). She and Landon owned both radio and TV stations.

In a letter to John Slack dated February 7, 1978, Ned wrote that he had received fairly reliable information that the National Association of Broadcasters did not intend to put forth its best effort to oppose repeal of the Lea Act. Ned figured that the broadcasters didn't think it necessary. (Apparently, he wasn't going to be jailed by a broadcaster's complaint or endure a "character assassination" like Jimmy Petrillo.) Ned, however, believed that the well-funded broadcast lobby— empowered with "the news" and armed with the effective, though subtle, "power of omission"—was the strongest lobby in Washington. He knew that a *little* opposition, from what is sometimes referred to as "the fourth branch of Government," could squash repeal like an unwanted bug at their dinner table.

But no matter, union officers Ned Guthrie and Hank Armantrout were suited up and traveling together on a plane to Washington, flying at what they thought to be seven or eight hundred feet above the Washington Monument. "You could almost reach out and touch it," Ned marveled. "It was a wonderful day and—I know this is a little corny but—we shook hands right over the top of the Washington Monument, and swore that we were going to stay with this until we got this thing repealed."

Ned carried a booklet with all of the locals and their officers listed. He'd go to telephones in congressional hallways—dimes handy—and call the local within the constituency of his targeted legislator. He'd say to the president or any other available officer, "Call and tell Representative (whoever) that *your* representative is in the lobby of his office, and he has an issue that is a dire necessity for the well-being of your membership."

This tactic usually worked like a charm to gain access to legislators, but there was hell to pay in the committees. Ned learned that you don't wait for your turn to get your bill heard. You must fight for it—and he did, doggedly lobbying the communications committees in both Houses of Congress for a period of almost six years. Musicians had a "labor" problem and a "free speech" (civil liberties) issue, the likes of which usually fell under the jurisdiction of committees other than the communications committees. The real problem lay in the conflicting interests of aggressive corporations and special-interest groups that glommed on to any communications bill to tack on endless amendments until controversy killed the bill. From "Ma Bell" to cable and network conglomerates, they twisted arms and proceeded through front and back doors with fistfuls of PAC money. It was a circus of interests. The years flew by—each year bringing with it some glimmer of hope to be dashed as another congressional session came to a close. The following year there would be another "charge up the Hill" to get a new number for the bill and have it reintroduced. Ned wasn't getting any younger, and it was a grind that would wear anybody down.

The process jumped decidedly ahead during the latter part of 1978, when Ned Guthrie was finally granted a hearing with the Senate Subcommittee on Communications. On June 13th of the following year, Ned started out testifying humbly enough.[36] It was the first of several opportunities to address the legislators in committee. He was prepared—readied like a cocked pistol, and his own good guy-bad guy team.

In a somewhat high tone of voice and sounding very West Virginian, Ned, smiling warmly at the lawmakers, said, "Hello neighbors, I'm from West Virginia and I've been a professional musician since 1929, when I started out in Harlan, Kentucky. My first broadcast was from the New River State College . . ." His testimony formed a subtle, slightly cranky crescendo as he was saying, ". . . but in *twelve* minutes time it is hard to tell what happened in the last thirty-three years. WHY, SIR!" Guthrie suddenly boomed, "how *dare* the Congress of the United States deprive me and my daughter over there and her students and her twelve-year-old daughter—my granddaughter Virginia Mitchel—from the opportunity of expressing themselves on the television, on the radio, and in their local communities to the exclusion of the syndicated programs!" Later asserting that syndication was *the* problem, Guthrie continued to say, "We're U.S. Citizens." His voice softened to plead, "Let us musicians. . . . We are loving people. We don't hate people. We won't give people trouble. We're here to create happiness. Allow us the same access to our marketplace as you allow a plumber to his."

DPE Director Jack Golodner, who had appeared earlier before the legislators to lobby for a "performance right in sound recordings," helped Ned by throwing in a good word for repeal. Mark Massagli was there, and his testimony no doubt pricked up some legislative ears when he said, "In my lectures on collective bargaining at the University (Las Vegas), I always make it a point to raise the Lea Act prohibitions as it is the only example I know that proscribes collective bargaining."

At House communications hearings Ned maintained, "The broadcasters are not interested in wasting their time and equipment to broadcast live music. It would upset their monopoly in distribution and be detrimental to their way of doing business on people's talents."[37]

Ned provided the committees with documentation and personal appearances by musicians. A bandleader named Buddy Davis had been vigorously threatened with bodily harm by a broadcaster for insisting on some airplay for his new tape. He had told the station manager, "You're using the public airways here, and you should give me some kind of public exposure!" Though Buddy (an African-American guitarist) didn't go into a racial "rap," he did say, "I have had a hard time as it is, but when they are going to throw me down the steps, and won't even play my record . . . ? And I get barred by law from even bargaining with them . . . ."[38]

A banjo, guitar, and mandolin picker with Flatt & Scruggs named Everett Lilly—who had been sought out by, and broadcast for, WJLS in Beckley, West Virginia—also testified, "I got booked up on the Hillbilly Shack in Boston one weekend," he said, "and they kept me seventeen years. I've gone to Japan three times, but when my boy got killed in an automobile accident two years ago . . . . So, my wife and I and my family wanted to come back to West Virginia. I came back here and they won't even play my records. And I helped open the station up!"

Everett Lilly also accompanied Ned to see Senator Byrd and to lobby Congressman Nick Rahall. While they were talking with Senator Byrd, the Senator received a telephone call they thought to be from either Egypt or Air Force One. President Carter was informing his Senate Majority Leader that he had convinced Sadat to make peace with Israel. Byrd shared this information with the two musicians, perhaps distinguishing them as the first civilians privy to this peace accord. Ned states with great satisfaction, "Byrd told us that, then went right back to discussing *our* bill." Their efforts also paid off with Representative Nick Rahall, an owner of two radio stations in West Virginia. He later rose on the Floor and said, "I'm a broadcaster, but I firmly believe that musicians should be treated equally. They ought to have the right to seek collective bargaining without threat of imprisonment."[39]

Adding a performer's, mother's, and teacher's viewpoint, Ned's daughter Diane testified, as did Henry Kaiser, the retired chief counsel of the Federation. Though he didn't say much, Ned notes, "That's because it's easy to tell right from wrong."

Kaiser didn't expect to be paid for his legal expertise by Ned's repeal committee. Now deceased, Kaiser's case was rejected by the Supreme Court in 1947, but his brilliant career aided the efforts of over fifty unions. It was he who beat the Justice Department's injunction procedure against the recording ban in the early 1940's "canned" music wars. His help was invaluable when Senator Byrd set up a meeting between Kaiser, Guthrie, and the Assistant Secretary of Labor, William Hodggood. This meeting was Ned's first glimmer of hope

Top: Henry Kaiser, Ned Guthrie, Mark Massagli
Mattox Photography
Bottom: Representative Lionel Van Deerlin, Ned Guthrie,
Hank Armantrout
Photograph by Gail S. Rebhan

for a foot in the door to the Oval Office.

Ned was sent by John Slack to Harley Staggers, the House Commerce Committee Chairman. They set up a meeting. Hank Armantrout was also in attendance to hear Slack tell Staggers, "I didn't know anything like this could be on the books. Why don't you call your staff and I'll walk Ned and Hank over there and make sure they know where to go."

It was unusual, but Staggers summoned his legal aide and said, "Brian, I want you to *listen* to them!" Brian Moir—a sharp thirty-eight-year-old lawyer who had been with Staggers for twelve years—kept thumbing through several record books as Ned was explaining the Lea Act to him. Ned paused and said accusingly, "You're not listening!"

"Yes I am!" retorted Moir, and quickly looked up at Ned to ask, "This has been on the books for thirty years?"

"It sure has," replied Ned, "since 1946."

"Well," Moir said, "I didn't know about this."

"Of course not," giggled Guthrie. "You're too damn young to know about it."

Brian came around his desk and told Ned and Hank, "Now, I'm not an advocate, but you can shoot this one down. I can't tell you I'm for it, but you can really do it. It's mind-boggling. Congress should *never* have done this!"

John Slack had steered Ned well. In Charleston, John telephoned him at his home on a Sunday morning to say, "If you can meet me tomorrow morning before the eight o'clock plane for about ten minutes, I want to talk to you." Ned went to the Kanawha Airport and sat down with his political mentor. Slack instructed, "If you do these things, you'll succeed: These 'birds' on the Hill pay more attention to 'back home' than they do the AFL-CIO, or anything else. If you go at it that way—then you'll get it."

It was timely advice, for within a few days John Slack died

suddenly and unexpectedly in Alexandria, Virginia—one day before his sixty-fifth birthday. He had served Congress for eleven years, and he was Ned's friend. Ned claims, "That goes back to that rock that was coming at me from across the river. Someone was looking out for what I was trying to do."

On the 23rd of September in 1980, Representative Van Deerlin from the Commerce Committee introduced a comprehensive communications reform bill. He rose on the floor of the House and said, "Mr. Speaker, I move to suspend the rules . . . to amend the Communications Act . . . to provide that the Federal Communications Commission, in considering applications for a renewal of broadcasting station licenses, shall not take into account any ownership interests of the applicant in other communications media, and for other purposes, as amended." The main common carrier issue involved the pros and cons of a monopolistic ownership of both a radio station *and* a newspaper in a given community. "Other purposes" referred to the Lea Act repeal and a second common carrier issue—a dispute over FCC licensing for stations that had been denied to both Delaware and New Jersey for a period of some twenty years.

Debates over the common carriers dragged on and on. The FCC made the claim that existing network monopolies were *good* for the public interest. Some legislators disagreed. Others disputed the "suspension of rules" that glued the three issues into one. Approximately eighty percent of the House floor debate was centered on the common carrier issues. The remaining time revolved around the Lea Act—interspersed with some heartfelt comments made about John Slack. Representatives Akaka (also a musician) and Matsui got in some good "licks" for repeal. Matsui pointed out that the Lea Act had a "chilling effect on musicians' and actors' freedom of expression." One opponent to repeal made one fleeting reference to featherbedding. Other than that, the musicians and their problems were of small concern as debate time ran out on the floor. It all boiled down to the vote, and the motion was rejected.

As had happened so many times in committee, repeal was dying on the vine—but Van Deerlin saved it by consulting with the Republican opposition. He then received unanimous consent on the floor to refer the bill to his Committee on Interstate and Foreign Commerce.

Prior to this action, when Ned's bill was debated on the floor, three "big shots" from the NAB had ridiculed him. They thought they had blocked his bill from reaching the floor of the House, chiding him with, "Better luck next time!" Ned spotted them shortly after the vote on the floor and, sure enough, one of them came at him with another verbal cut.

Ned coolly offered the same thing he had told them in committee, "Don't worry, I'll be back." Their arrogance sometimes got under his skin because he *was* experiencing setbacks.

Van Deerlin had notified President Fuentealba that the Judiciary Committee was processing the decodification of some criminal laws. The Lea Act's criminal penalties had prompted the Judiciary to claim jurisdiction over the repeal bill from communications. A meeting was scheduled. Ned requested and received permission to attend it, and flew to Washington. His hopes were up. He was excited. When he arrived, he was informed that two legislators and Van Deerlin had met the previous day for ten minutes—long enough to vote down repeal on the basis that further deliberations were needed.

Another setback came when Bob Guthrie (no relation to Ned), Assistant Director of the Department of Professional Employees, heard about the Judiciary claiming jurisdiction and requested information from the Federation. As it had in

1976, the DPE was pushing for a performance right in sound recordings, and tried to combine performance rights with repeal. Ned was all for performers having copyright protection, but combining them was something he quickly termed a "Bay of Pigs approach." Ned knew that it would fail, and it did. He believed that Communications—for better or worse—was the only committee likely to take an in-depth look at the Lea Act.

All through this fight, Ned had suffered from arthritic knees. In fact, he had experienced knee problems since he fell in New Orleans while tussling with the crook. His doctor prescribed rest, and recommended surgery for his pronounced limp—so Ned bought a cane!—and used it as a pointer, dramatically directing attention to the Bill of Rights. He bore pain like a "chip off the ol' block" and went about his usual freight train way of doing things—but now limping, hobbling, and leaning on his cane as he did.

It was through John Slack (whose loss engendered calls on the floor to make repeal of the Lea Act a memorial tribute) that Ned found "grass roots" lobbying as the way to press on. It could generate a considerable amount of union power otherwise nonexistent, and could be used to accomplish things other than this repeal, such as a performance right. There wasn't anything new about grass roots lobbying, but it was new enough to the musicians' union. Not since Weber's failed "talkie" campaign in the 1920's had such a broadly based action been initiated by musicians.

The introduction of Ned's bill, springing it out of subcommittee to the full committee, steering it through committee to report it out, and scheduling the floor debate required one or more legislators every step of the way. Guthrie's little crew of frontline people were obliged to contact union officers residing within the congressional districts of targeted legislators. His committee could reach into most every local in the country for help, and he now had the major offices in the Federation involved—awaiting his directives. *The International Musician* (official voice of the Federation) remained receptive to his and Armantrout's writings. The strings on the Federation's "money bag," however, remained tightly drawn—officially ignoring Guthrie's obvious need to finance what had become one of "the Federation's" major campaigns.

Ned's committee was put to a hard test when President Tony Granata of the Cleveland Local accompanied Ned to visit Congressman Motti. Motti scheduled the hearing that materialized in the Harley Staggers's committee. Ned's committee received a jolt when Subcommittee Chairman Van Deerlin scheduled this "pow-wow" for the following day— knowingly leaving the musicians' lobby in a dilemma. Guthrie's special "Attack Committee" consisted of Roy Pittman, Frank Thompson, Hank Armantrout, and himself. They had eighteen hours to contact forty-two legislators through their constituents in locals scattered all over America, explain the bill, and prod officials to pressure their congressmen—and do it *now!* They hit the phones while the other Guthrie from the DPE contacted his people, and the push was on. Eighteen exhausting hours later the forty-two legislators were cognizant, if not in complete understanding, of the bill. The broadcast lobby wasn't exactly caught flat-footed—though probably surprised that Ned's Attack Committee was that effective and had that kind of firepower. They retaliated by trying to tack amendments on Ned's bill to kill it, forcing Ned and his crew to contact each and every legislator—"one more once."

Harley Staggers sat on the bill until the climate was more favorable for passage before springing it to the floor, and it took constituent pressure (plus political influence from Staggers, Governor Rockefeller, *and* the New York State AFL-CIO) to spur Tip O'Neil into reporting the bill out of committee on the suspension of rules calendar. An objection was immediately voiced by a congressman from Ohio. The Cleveland Local quickly stomped that fire out and, after four solid weeks of this scrimmaging, the repeal bill passed through the House of Representatives on October 1, 1980. It passed with a voice vote, and despite the concerted efforts made against it, there was oddly not one vote voiced in opposition. Cheers and clapping were heard coming out of the peanut gallery where a handful of musicians had lodged themselves for the House show. Roy and his mother Anne Pittman were there, and were recognized from the floor.

Ned thought he had won. Then, a Republican congressman from Ohio motioned for a five-day waiting period for members to revise their remarks. The red flag was up again, and one of the lobbyists for the broadcasters couldn't resist taking another cheap shot at Guthrie. The bill did pass—but Ned didn't celebrate because the war wasn't over.

Repeal now went to the Senate, and it promised to be no less problematical there than it had been in the House. Ned couldn't help wondering what the broadcasters were up to. Their amendment game would undoubtedly move to the Senate, but Ned had a new war cry. This "no vote in dissension" provided him the opportunity to hollo, "IT'S ADVANCE PUBLICITY! REPEAL WILL FLY!"[40]

A bill entitled the "Comprehensive Reform Bill" was pigeonholed in the Senate. On the one hundred and twenty-fifth page of its one hundred and twenty-nine pages was a clause to repeal the Lea Act. Ned's committee *had* conjured up a "clean" bill (without amendments). The problem was keeping it that way when it hit the Senate floor as dupes of the broadcasters wielded their amendments. That happened like clockwork, and a bipartison compromise bill also emerged to muddy the waters. Senator Byrd and some other legislators wanted to vote on a clean bill, but an amendment of some shape or form appeared imminent. Senator Hollings, the Communications' Chairman, countered for Ned by exercising his right to refer the bill to his subcommittee. It was locked in there from October 2nd to November 12th.

Ned's committee was again in a sweat in November of 1980 fighting a barrage of amendment attacks that kept it extremely busy. In the midst of telephone campaigns and paper wars, a huge breakthrough came when President Vern Swingle of the Albuquerque Local, along with the membership of the New Mexico Symphony, prevailed on Senator Schmidt—a conservative "tough nut to crack." During the last congressional session, Schmidt had sent a letter to the Republican Policy Committee stating his intention to tack on a broadcast amendment to the repeal bill. It was sabotage, and his letter was the clincher that forced Holling's protective move to temporarily bury the bill in committee. Constituent pressure induced Mr. Schmidt to retrieve his letter, however, and his recapitulation apparently prompted Senator Goldwater to turn full circle on repeal. Following his example, most other conservative legislators fell in line. The Eugene Local in Oregon garnered the support of the Minority Ranking Member of the Senate Communications Committee. He scheduled the bill for Senate consideration. A senator from New Jersey tried to attach an amendment that would give WOR-TV's charter to his state. New Jersey constituents persuaded him to cool it. There were other fires to put out, and another off-the-wall comment out of a broadcaster's mouth hit Guthrie in the ear. Fed up with the opposition's skullduggery—he *stormed* into the dragon's den.

Confronting a ranking counsel to Senator Schmidt's Minority Segment of the Communications Committee in a charged but civil exchange, Guthrie made it clear that he wanted his bill to pass, insisting, "That *is* the way it's going to be!" The legislative assistant brandished two or three new amendments, then (perhaps realizing that there was no way he was going to get rid of Guthrie) said, "You want me to get my senator to withhold the amendment passed—*then the Democrats get all the credit!*"

Ned told him, "I'll made sure they get the proper recognition that Republicans deserve—and we'll *publish* it!"

Again, as in the House, there was no floor opposition when the Senate repeal bill passed the Senate on November 21st.

Within a few days, the bill was brought up again by Senator Byrd, the Majority Leader. Minority Leader Howard Baker, who was respectful of his country musician constituents in Tennessee, offered no objection—and hearing none, Byrd's move was successful. The Senate had passed the repeal by voice vote. It was late at night when Senator Byrd then made the motion to lay the motion "to reconsider" on the table. (The "table" was his! He was the Majority Leader of the Senate.) The chairman said, "Without objection, so ordered," and quickly slammed the gavel.

Ned had done everything that he could in Washington, and had returned home to Charleston. He had just finished supper when Byrd called him and announced, "I have good news! The musicians ought to have a statue made of you. The repeal passed the Senate!"

Within a few days, the bill was sent to the White House for President Carter's signature. In 1946, "Give 'em hell Harry" Truman had signed the Lea Act into existence. Would President Jimmy Carter sign its repeal in 1980? Ned thought so, but pressure had to be applied to the White House. Carter had lost the election and was leaving office. If for any reason he didn't sign the bill, Ned would be back at the drawing board, and all bets would be off. "I got scared," admits Ned. "Man, all that power the president has. All that effort, and everything down to just *one* person!"

Days went by and no word came from the Oval Office. Ned was becoming a nervous wreck. His eating and sleeping patterns were thrown off, and he took to pacing the floor of his living room—nonstop in three and four hour spurts. Ned the "pussycat" around the house was getting crabby. It was the first time he felt real political pressure, and fell into a state of anxiety. He telephoned people in Georgia (where Carter is from) who played in the Atlanta Symphony and others, urging them to call, write, or send telegrams to the President. He called Governor Rockefeller, who had worked with Carter. (Guthrie says that Rockefeller passed the coal miners' true-blue test.) Ned also called Senator Percy of Illinois (Rockefeller's father-in-law). He contacted everybody he could think of. As far as he could tell, a barrage of telegrams, letters, and telephone calls inundated Carter's office invoking nothing but a continuing silence. It got down to a matter of a days before Carter was history when Ned made a panic call to Congressman Harley Staggers and blurted out, "Mr. Staggers! We've come this far and the President hasn't signed that bill!"

"You mean he hasn't signed it yet?" Staggers responded. "I'll call the White House and tell him to *sign* the damn bill!" A man of his word, Staggers let the White House know the importance of the legislation.

Whatever did the trick, on the 8th day of December in 1980, President Carter's signature on Bill H.R. 4892 struck down the law that had all but killed live music broadcasts in America. No longer could a broadcaster's complaint incarcerate a musician in a federal penitentiary, and an amendment to the Copyright Act to provide performers a performance royalty was now a realistic legislative objective. Perhaps best understood as an unfair "trade regulation act" that placed the right of broadcasters to make a profit over musicians' civil rights, the Lea Act was repealed for its unconstitutionality. When Guthrie first received the news from Senator Byrd, the first thing that came out of his mouth was, "Thank God it was repealed while Jimmy Petrillo is still alive!"

Ned Guthrie never gave an inch on musicians' rights. In the *International Musician* he wrote:

> ". . . Democrats were in the best position to help us and they did. The Republicans were in a position to stop us as time was running short, but they did not—they helped us. Much credit should go to Senate Majority Leader Byrd and Senate Minority Leader Baker for their cooperation in restoring to musicians our rights under the Constitution. It was not a political gesture, it was a gesture of Americanism by both sides."

In retrospect, Ned muses, "In Washington politics, you don't get what you deserve. You get what you can *negotiate,* and that generally calls for a compromise."[41]

January 8, 1981

To Ned Guthrie

It was with great pleasure that I signed into law H.R. 4892, which repeals the Lea Act, section 506 of the Communications Act of 1934. I understand from Congressman Harley Staggers that you worked for several years toward the enactment of this measure. You can be proud of your persistence and pleased with the results of your labors.

In grateful recognition of your role in the development of this bill, I want you to have a ceremonial copy of the Act. May it serve as a reminder of your good work.

With best wishes,

Sincerely,

Jimmy Carter

Mr. Ned H. Guthrie, President
Charleston Musicians Union, Local 136
American Federation of Musicians
1562 Kanawha Boulevard, East
Charleston, West Virginia 25311

[CHAPTER 138]
AN ACT
To amend title V of the Communications Act of 1934 so as to prohibit certain coercive practices affecting radio broadcasting. April 16, 1946
[S. 63] Public Law 344

COERCIVE PRACTICES AFFECTING BROADCASTING

Sec. 506.(a) It shall be unlawful, by the use or implied threat of the use of force, violence, intimidation, or duress, or by the use or express or implied threat of the use of other means, to coerce, compel, or constrain or attempt to coerce, compel or constrain a licensee—

(Employment of excess employees)

(1) to employ or agree to employ, in connection with the conduct of broadcasting business of such licensee, any person or persons in excess of the number of employees needed by such licensee to perform actual services; or

(Payment in lieu of giving employment)

(2) to pay or give or agree to pay or give any money or other thing of value in lieu of giving, or on account of failure to give, employment to any person or persons, in connection with the conduct of the broadcasting business of such licensee, in excess of the number of employees needed by such licensee to perform actual services; or

(Payment more than once)

(3) to pay or agree to pay more than once for services performed in connection with the conduct of the broadcasting business of such licensee; or

(Payment for services not performed)

(4) to pay or give or agree to pay or give any money or other thing of value for services, in connection with the conduct of the broadcasting business of such licensee, which are not to be performed; or

(Noncommercial educational or cultural programs)

(5) to refrain, or agree to refrain, from broadcasting or from permitting the broadcasting of a noncommercial educational or cultural program in connection with which the participants receive no money or other thing of value for their services, or their actual expenses, and such licensee neither pays nor gives any money or other thing of value for the privilege of broadcasting such program nor receives any money or other thing of value on account of the broadcasting of such program; or

(Radio communication originating outside the U.S.)

(6) to refrain, or agree to refrain, from broadcasting or permitting the broadcasting of any radio communication originating outside the United States.

(b) It shall be unlawful, by the use or express or implied threat of the use of force, violence, intimidation or duress, or by the use or express or implied threat of the use of other means, to coerce, compel or constrain or attempt to coerce, compel or constrain a licensee or any other person—

(Payment of exaction for using recordings, etc.)

(1) to pay or agree to pay any exaction for the privilege of, or on account of, producing, preparing, manufacturing, selling, buying, renting, operating, using, or maintaining recordings, transcriptions, or mechanical, chemical, or electrical reproductions, or any other articles, equipment, machines, or materials, used or intended to be used in broadcasting or in the production, preparation, performance, or representation of a program or programs for broadcasting; or

(Restriction of production, etc.)

(2) to accede to or impose any restriction upon such production, preparation, manufacture, sale, purchase, rental, operation, use, or maintenance, if such restriction is for the purpose of preventing or limiting the use of such articles, equipment, machines, or materials in broadcasting or in the production, preparation, performance, or presentation of a program or programs for broadcasting; or

(Payment of exaction for program previously broadcast.)

(3) to pay or agree to pay any exaction on account of the broadcasting, by means of recordings or transcriptions, of a program previously broadcast, payment having been made, or agreed to be made, for the services actually rendered in the performance of such program.

(Enforcement of contract right.)

(c) The provisions of subsection (a) or (b) of this section shall not be held to make unlawful the enforcement or attempted enforcement, by means lawfully employed, of any contract right heretofore or hereafter existing or of any legal obligation heretofore or hereafter incurred or assumed.

(Penalty provision.)

(d) Whoever willfully violates any provision of subsection (a) or (b) of this section shall, upon conviction thereof, be punished by imprisonment for not more than one year or by a fine of not more than $1,000, or both.

("Licensee.")

(e) As used in this section the term "licensee" includes the owner or owners, and the person or persons having control or management of the radio station in respect of which a station license was granted.

Tom Lee, Cosimo Abato, Victor Fuentealba,
Ned Guthrie, Senator Byrd
U. S. Senate Photograph

Conclusion

An offspring of the "news," the Lea Act wasn't "newsworthy" when it was repealed, and has been omitted from discussion on the commercial airways. Though its adverse effects continue to plague the musicians' business, and the underlying problem of patent, copyright, and restraint of trade remains unresolved, the Lea Act is seldom mentioned in literature.

Ned's victory, nevertheless, was for union and non-union musicians alike. It didn't go entirely unnoticed. His friend and ex-partner, Jim Beane, says, "I argued with Ned about something or other most every day, but after being his partner for twenty some years and all, he just has a big heart—and he's gullible. You can just bullshit him to death, but he often knows what you're thinking about before you start. That was necessary for the people he had to fool with. There isn't another man in the U.S. that could have done what he did. He would not quit! Ned just got involved with this Local. He didn't always do it right. He just did it the way he did it. He just wasn't bullshit."

Ned received a letter of congratulations from Jimmy Carter noting that he should be "proud of his persistence and pleased with the results of his labors." A letter from Harley Staggers recognized Ned's "persistence and energy," and he also received recognition from as far away as Japan. Henry Kaiser, Ned's counsel, wrote to say, "What you did single-handedly surpasses my entire Washington experience." That was quite a statement coming from Henry—though understandable. Repealing a law is decidedly more difficult than creating new legislation. Repeal of a law that the Supreme Court had already ruled to be constitutionally sound is a *remarkable* accomplishment. When Ned wanted support from Willy Nelson for national legislation, the president and secretary-treasurer of the Fort Worth Local, Ray Hair, advised him to talk to Nelson's drummer, Paul English. Ned boarded one of Willy Nelson's band buses—the one marked "ME AND PAUL" on the front of it—and Ned, Paul, and Willy had a long chat. After Ned left, Paul telephoned Ray Hair. Like Senator Byrd, Ray thought a statue should be made of Ned, but Paul felt that wouldn't be enough. Thinking big in Texas, they came up with a name for Ned Guthrie: "The Musicians' Abraham Lincoln." That "handle" might stick if musicians realize their *freedom* to negotiate a living with the tenants of *their* public airways.

In June of 1981, Jay Victor of *Nation's Labor* magazine in Chicago ran an exuberant article on Guthrie entitled, "IN MEMORIAM, THE LEA ACT—a Mongoloid, born April 16, 1946, died Dec. 8, 1980." He writes, ". . . where all other attempts to wipe the Lea Act off the books ended in failure, his won the day. It's a reenactment of the David and Goliath theme in modern dress, with a balding clarinetist wielding the slingshot that finally subdued the obdurate giant. . . ." Victor's pen punished "those who had sneered at 'Guthrie's

Folly'" and "changed their posture only when the smell of victory was in the air."[42] Ned Guthrie, however, is grateful for *any* help he received. He often makes the point, "The power is with the membership."

A Lea Act honor roll (admittedly incomplete and in no special order) would include John Slack, Marty Emerson, Hank Armantrout, Brian Moir, Buddie Davis, Tom Kenny, Kelly Castleberry, Hal Bailey, Mark Massagli, John D. Rockefeller IV, Norman Fagen, Harley Staggers, Ned Massey, Mike Seigliano, Senator Byrd, and a host of others. But Ned thinks it is doubtful that "labor" would have gotten to first base with the "money people" in Washington without the help of Roy Pittman. Ned says, "He bridged that gap, and carried musicians over the bridge of troubled waters." (Roy continued to help musicians after the repeal of the Lea Act, and persuaded Rockefeller to award Guthrie the status of "Distinguished West Virginian." Roy Pittman died at age thirty-five in 1987 of a rare disease called myasthenia gravis.)

Sometime in 1982, Ned received a visit from Kelly Castleberry. Kelly had become an International Representative of the Field Staff for Fuentealba's presidential office, a job that required traveling between Locals. Wanting to return with his family to Charleston to live, he had set his eye on winning Ned's job as president of the Charleston Local. Kelly was quite the politician. He told Ned that he wanted his job, but that he didn't want to run against him.

Ned looked at him and growled, "You better not, I'll *beat* your ass!" (Ned still maintains that Kelly was just "whistlin' Dixie," meaning "it won't work.")

"Now just hold on," laughed Kelly. "I think I can get Fuentealba to make you our representative in Washington."

"You *do?*" questioned Ned, raising an eyebrow at the notion of it.

In due time, Ned was summoned to New York by Fuentealba, who had arranged for the Federation to pay Ned's travel expenses. Realizing the importance of national legislation, Fuentealba offered Ned a committee. *Oh boy,* thought Ned, *a committee!* He smelled a rat. This didn't sound like a paying job. Ned diplomatically told President Fuentealba, "I don't want to work with you. I want to work *for* you!"

A little later, on the ninth of January, 1983, Fuentealba appointed Guthrie under modest salary to the post of "National Legislative Director" of the American Federation of Musicians. As the first appointed official to serve under this title, Guthrie has survived changes of presidency from Fuentealba to Marty Emerson, and currently serves under President Massagli's administration. Guthrie gave up his local office in 1982, and is now President Emeritus of Charleston Local 136.

The West Virginia Division of Culture and History put Ned's name up for induction into the West Virginia Labor Hall of Honor.[43] On the 27th of June in 1987, Ned Guthrie took his place in labor history in the company of Arnold Miller, Mother Jones, the Walter Reuther Family, and other honored labor leaders. President Richard Knapp of the Labor History Association presented the award at the Ramada Inn in South Charleston. Gladys was there—as was Ned Guthrie, Jr. (whose band "The Rondells," was the first live band on American Bandstand in 1958). Ned's half-brother, Lt. Colonel Fleetwood Guthrie, was also in proud attendance. The Charleston Local provided an orchestra, and Fuentealba and Kelly Castleberry (who by that time had become secretary-treasurer to the Federation) flew in from New York. Tom Bailey (president of the Charleston Local), Sam Folio (a member of the Federation's Executive Board), and the Earl of Elkview made speeches. The Earl presented Ned with a T-shirt, proclaiming him to be a member of "The West Virginia Comin' Back Hallelujah Marchin' Band." Ned Guthrie was seventy-three years young when he was called to the podium after his induction. Characteristically he told everybody, "This is not a wake. I just got started."

The word "tenacious" is inadequate to describe Guthrie's fervor. Working to establish Union presence, he was the kind of union man that would, and did, card Elvis Presley's band minutes before show time. Ned feels that someone should *always* be proud to show their card, and he was known for carding most anyone and everyone, including celebrities and even President Yasushi Ashida (national president of the Japanese musicians' union)— a polite man. Ned let out a little giggle while recalling that this high official, who was a visiting guest at a convention, had searched everywhere in his pockets and wallet. Embarrassed, President Ashida gave Ned the old excuse (with an added variation), "I left it on the dresser, *in Tokyo.*" Knowing who he was, Ned *half*-jokingly made him promise to mail back a photostat of his card when he returned to Japan—and he did!

Ned watched his talented children and grandchildren drift away from making music for a living, a result of inequitable laws. He was highly motivated, and remained an effective president of his local in Charleston during the eight years it took him to get the Lea Act repealed.

Guthrie brags, "I beat the Supreme Court on this one! It got me started, and I can't stop!" Pointing the way to national legislation, Ned has walked the Halls of Congress for eighteen years on behalf of the American musician, and introduced grass roots politics into his union. In 1991, grass roots saved the Music Performance Trust Fund.

Despite such success, the director of the FCC, at a meeting in his office in Washington, told Ned, "Just because you repealed the Lea Act doesn't mean you're going to go back to work on radio."

"That's what we're going to do!" Ned countered.

"The National Association of Broadcasters will come after you like a tiger," scoffed this "watchdog of the public airways."

"Well," retorted Ned, "we'll just shoot that tiger between the eyes."

Nevertheless, that tiger has been elusive. As yet, there is no national plan of action initiated by the Federation to recapture the airways. President Massagli says, "What the repeal itself has effected is difficult to measure . . . with this changing industry there may still be a day when the absence of that terrible legislation will provide us the rights in a very significant way to represent professional musicians."

The first union action taken following repeal was an immediate response from the San Francisco Local. As the story goes, an official spotted and identified a union musician employed by a radio station as a disc jockey. Following repeal, the Local notified the station management that it was ready to bargain. For what it's worth, it worked and they made it stick. There was some short-lived talk of taking the disc jockeys into the union, presumably after the musician-DJ received a raise in pay.

In West Virginia, Guthrie convinced the musicians in his local that there was money to be made on the airways, now that the broadcasters didn't have a "dagger" pointed at them. Many people, including Norman Fagen and Andy Ridenour, became involved in cooperative negotiations, and the outcome was "Mountain Stage," now broadcast live every Sunday on West Virginia Public Radio.

Some commercial broadcasters in West Virginia initially pooh-poohed the idea of presenting local talent on radio, but Mountain Stage has been well received. It is now picked up by over one hundred PBS stations around the country. Broadcasters prefer their "star system," which locks out all but less than one percent of the musicians from the public airways, their major market. We in America are consequently ignorant of over ninety-nine percent of our own music. Public recognition of this deprivation could ignite remedial legislation, and there are FCC rulings, which, though not enforced, support reinstatement of live broadcasting—as a "public service."[44]

"We're American citizens," reminds Guthrie. "My ghost will do it if I don't. We're that much farther ahead than we were before repeal. The challenge is there. But with musicians you have to understand that it all started back in King Arthur's court, and before. The king would say, 'Stand over there until I snap my fingers. Then come out tumbling and play good music—*or I'll chop your head off!*' I've heard the phrase, 'Those goddamn musicians!' all my life. That attitude often shows through, and it is difficult for legislators to fathom that maybe—*just maybe*—something might be wrong."

At the ripe old age of eighty-two, Ned Guthrie keeps making octogenarian comebacks. It can be said that he sacrificed his knees for repeal of a law. Years of ignoring his doctor's advice eventually led to a double knee operation at age seventy-nine. It was followed by a stroke and numerous other complications—and more operations. During times when he was hospitalized, some people were concerned about not only Ned's health, but also his ability to carry on. Then they would receive a telephone call from Ned and be issued a directive, no less, and usually find it difficult to put to rest one of Ned's lengthy dissertations on the intricacies of national legislation. The first time Ned was hospitalized, Kelly's only tight-lipped comment was, "Ned will have a job with the Federation as long as he wants it." Indeed, Ned appears to be the only official who has the knowledge and rapport with enough personalities in Congress to get the job done. If nothing else, he has the designated time. Legislative initiatives do take time, but Ned spends as much time lobbying musicians as he does the legislature. He insists, "That is *not* right!"

Ned Humphries Guthrie—a musicians' knight if there ever was one—is respected, admired, and well-loved by a great many people. He has also been avoided, and has enemies. He's been shot at and sued twice in the line of duty, has received bad press, and is a person many Charlestonians would say is as ornery and obnoxious as ever. He says:

> I love this work, but if I had it to do all over again, I'd rather work among wild animals. I never saw any wild animals that didn't give each other a break. So, when I go into the next world, I'll be some sort of curator for the most beautiful things that the Lord ever made. I do love animals. And I love flowers. I raise a few, but I guess you don't love anybody or anything like you love your wife. There's a song out about that. It says something about how 'you were always there when I needed you . . . .'[45]

THE END

NED AND GLADYS
PHOTOGRAPH BY MICHAEL KELLER
COURTESY OF WEST VIRGINIA DIVISION OF CULTURE & HISTORY

Notes

1. West Virginia was formerly Virginia. In the agony of a "Blue-Gray tradition," there were two years of skirmishes when the Union Army invaded mineral rich western Virginia, initially to take control of the railroad that came through Clarksburg. The first Union defeat was at Scary Creek in Saint Albans. But, in a war of errors, the Confederacy abandoned the area, and the North prevailed to establish a military line across two-thirds of the state. A book about these skirmishes is entitled, *"The War Diaries, the 1861 Kanawha Valley Campaign,"* by David L. Phillips, Gauley Mount Press, 1990. On June 20, 1863—without the consent of the citizens—President Lincoln created the State of West Virginia by proclamation and signature. Corporate out of state controls over the natural *and* the political resources of West Virginia were established by the 1900's. The history of this statehood—and the corporate abuse of the inhabitants since then—is neatly reflected in a college "moonshine" drinking toast: "Here's to West Virginia! Long may she live! The South couldn't keep her, and the North didn't want her—the bastard of a political rape!"

2. *Charleston Gazette,* 11/1/1990.

3. *Ibid.*

4. *Ibid.*

5. *Ibid.*

6. Courts ruled musicians to be independent contractors in the late 1960's and 1970's. Leaders and solo acts are being classified as "management," therefore not entitled to union representation. Pending rulings by courts and the National Labor Relations Board (NLRB), or a proposed amendment to the Taft-Hartley in the 1990's (something that Ned has been working on for all of seven years), may decide the dispute between bookers and other employers

164

against musicians—to settle the question, "Who's the boss?" Ned Guthrie lobbies Congress to reclassify musicians as "employees." Though the proposed Live Performing Arts Labor Relations Act (LivePALRA) amendment that Ned lobbies does not affect taxes or bookkeeping for employers, opposition to amending the Taft-Hartley Act is vehement—but then, so is Guthrie.

7. *Charleston Gazette*, 11/1/1990.
8. *Radio Daily*, 2/3/1942, p. 13.
9. *The Musicians & Petrillo*, Robert Leiter, p. 134.
10. *Ibid.*
11. Letter from Mark Massagli, 4/3/1992, remembered from a conversation he had with Jimmy Petrillo sometime in the early 1980's.
12. *Wonderful Inventions*, Samuel Brylawski, Library of Congress, 1985, p. 365.
13. *Ibid.*
14. *Downbeat*, 11/1/1942, pp. 1, 13.
15. National Association of Broadcasters, *Special Bulletin*, 10/23/1942, No. 12.
16. *Broadcasting, Broadcast Advertising*, 10/26/1942, p. 60.
17. *Downbeat*, 8/1/1942, p. 10.
18. *Ibid.*
19. *Life*, 8/3/1942, p. 70.
20. *Current Biography*, 1940, p. 650.
21. *Collier's*, 1/9/1943, p. 29.
22. *Radio Daily*, 7/21/1942, pp. 1, 5.
23. *Wonderful Inventions*.
24. *Congressional Record*, 2/21/1942, p. 1550.
25. *Congressional Record*, 2/21/1942, p. 3248.
26. *Congressional Record*, 2/21/1942, p. 2822.
27. Id. at 1554, footnote in Henry Kaiser's brief to the Supreme Court in Lea vs. U.S., Mem. 331, US 833, 67 S ct 1513, 9 1.1846.
28. *Congressional Record*, House, 3/29/1946, p. 2822.
29. *Ibid.*
30. *Musicians & Petrillo*.
31. *Nation's Labor*.
32. *Minority Views* Report No. 1508, Part 2, 79th Congress, 2nd Session to accompany H.R. 5117, submitted 2/8/1946 by the Committee on Interstate and Foreign Commerce.
33. *Wonderful Inventions*.
34. Jay Victor, *Nation's Labor*, Vol. 11, and No. 6, 6/1981 and *Goldenseal, West Virginia Traditional Life*, Vol. 13, No. 3, Fall 1987, "Facing The Music" by Lori L. Henshey, p. 17.
35. *Nation's Labor*, Vol. 7, No. 11, 11/1977.
36. Amendments to the Communications Act of 1934, 6/13/1977, Subcommittee of the Committee on Commerce, Science, and Transportation, Part 4, Serial No. 96-45.
37. *Congressional Record*, 9/23/1980.
38. *House Communications*, 6/13/1980.
39. *Congressional Record*, 9/23/1980.

40. *International Musician,* 1/1981, p.1.

41. *Ibid.*

42. *Nation's Labor.*

43. The West Virginia Labor Hall of Honor is sponsored by the West Virginia Labor History Association to recognize individuals who make outstanding contributions to improve the quality of life of working people of West Virginia and the nation.

44. In Tampa Times Co. (10 R.R. 77, 127), the FCC said, "but because an applicant through its local live programming demonstrates his capacity to meet community needs and desires and serves as an outlet for local expression, we attach great weight to local live programming." Stated in Odessa Television Co. (11 R.R. 755, 773) determined "in evaluating the program proposals of an applicant, the amount of its proposed live programming serves best to demonstrate its ability to meet and fulfill the needs of the community involved." Tribune Co. (9 R.R. 719, 770c), designated live broadcasting to be "a positive responsibility . . . upon the licensee to make articulate the voices of the community." Matter of Applications of Loyola University, *et al.* (Docket No. 8936 *et al.*), in a comparative television proceeding involving applicants in the New Orleans' area, praised a successful applicant that had employed two staff orchestras at a radio station for promising to continue hiring musicians if it could obtain a license to operate a television station. It also criticized and refused to renew licensing to a radio applicant for not fulfilling a promise made to employ an orchestra. Courier Post Publishing Co. vs. FCC (104 F. 2d 213) designated the duty of local broadcasters to "utilize and develop local entertainment talent which the record indicates is available . . . ."

45. Joyce Davis Adams interviewed Ned Guthrie on 3/18, 10/27, and 11/16 in 1983. Her notes and a resulting article written by Lori L. Henshey in *Goldenseal,* Vol. 13, No. 3, Fall 1987, provided many stories and quotes that appear throughout this book—courtesy of the West Virginia Division of Culture & History.

Index

Index